The Guide to Translation and Localization

Preparing for the Global Marketplace

by

Copyright © 2004 by Lingo Systems

Copyright and Reprint Permissions: Abstracting is permitted with credit to the source. Libraries are permitted to photocopy isolated pages beyond the limits of US copyright law for private use of their patrons. For other copying, reprint, or publication permission write to Lingo Systems, 15115 SW Sequoia Parkway, Suite 200, Portland, Oregon 97224.

Library of Congress Number 2004095559
ISBN 0-9703948-2-9

Additional Copies can be ordered from:

Lingo Systems
15115 SW Sequoia Parkway
Suite 200
Portland, OR 97224

Tel: 800-878-8523
503-419-4856
FAX: 503-419-4873

www.lingosys.com
info@lingosys.com

Printed in the United States of America

Editorial Board:
Dan Johnson, Scott Ludwigsen, Dan Roth, Willy van Grunsven

Managing Editor:
Jeff Williams

Copy Editor:
Steve Heikkila

Art Director:
Roger Thompson

Staff Photos:
Donald E. Arney

Design:
Pete Landers

Contributing Writers:
Donald E. Arney, Nicole Benjamin, Barbara Bonnema, Perry Brooks, Ting Fan, Dan Johnson, Pete Landers, Scott Ludwigsen, Eric Manning, David Martin, Ursula Mühlhaus Moyer, Donna Parrish, Dan Roth, Ehren Schneider, Cristina Tacconi, Paul Trotter, Barbara Weiss, Chris van Grunsven, Willy van Grunsven, Cedric Vezinet, Laurel Wagers, Wasi Wahedi, Danielle Walker, Jeff Williams. And many thanks to all of our employees past and present who have contributed to the many editions of the Guidebook.

Trademark Information
Windows and Windows Help are trademarks of Microsoft Corporation. TRADOS Translator's Workbench for Windows is the registered trademark of TRADOS GmbH. Quark and QuarkXpress are registered trademarks of Quark, Inc. Adobe, Adobe Illustrator, Adobe Photoshop, Acrobat, FrameMaker, PageMaker, Adobe Type Manager, and PostScript are trademarks of Adobe Systems Inc., AuthorIT, Webworks, RoboHelp, Documentum, and Interwoven are trademarks of these individual products.

All other brand or product names, trademarks, service marks, and copyrights are the property of their respective owners.

The Guide to Translation and Localization was published using the AuthorIT single-source content management system.

Contact Information:
MultiLingual Computing
319 North First Avenue
Sandpoint, ID 83864

Tel: 208-263-8178
FAX: 208-263-6310

www.multilingual.com

Lingo Systems
15115 SW Sequoia Parkway
Suite 200
Portland, OR 97224

Tel: 800-878-8523
503-419-4856
FAX: 503-419-4873

www.lingosys.com
info@lingosys.com

Foreword

Donna Parrish
MultiLingual Computing, Inc.
Editor-in-Chief,
Publisher

It seems strange to be involved with international people and issues while working in Sandpoint, Idaho. That's one reason we were particularly pleased to cooperate with our "neighbors" in Oregon to work on this book. One thing I have found about the localization industry, you really do meet the nicest people—and they all have stories to tell. Just keep reading!

A member of our staff recently attended a local business meeting dealing with international marketing research. Conducted by a college marketing professor in a department of global commerce, the discussion centered around the fact that international products and documents must be translated and customized for their intended local markets. When our staff member suggested that what he was talking about was localization, the professor said something to this effect: "What a great word! Yes, that is exactly what I mean!"

So, here we are. The concept of localization is finally reaching the more general public, even if the term isn't.

At MultiLingual Computing, Inc., we try hard to get both the concepts and the terms out to people in and outside of this industry. *MultiLingual Computing & Technology*, our flagship magazine, provides a healthy mix of introductory articles for beginners, linguistic articles for translators and technical articles for engineers. Our free biweekly newsletter, *MultiLingual News*, keeps people up-to-date with new products, services and changes in the industry. Our website (www.multilingual.com) offers a searchable database of over 1200 industry resources, online articles, listings of events (such as Localization World), a blog and more.

Yes, we are an information source for people in the translation and localization industries. But when someone comes to MultiLingual who needs an introduction to the concepts and terms, we refer them to *The Guide to Translation and Localization*.

So we are very happy to join Lingo Systems in publishing this edition of the Guide. If you are new to the whole translation and localization arena, this book gives you a head start by examining industry-specific terms, choices you can make, tips on project planning, project management, quality assurance and production. It makes the whole process a little more doable without minimizing the challenges ahead. If you are an old hand in this industry, you will benefit by reviewing core concepts and reading case studies. And everyone enjoys the "Oops" entries!

Good luck in your international venture. Your success will be based on hard work, careful planning, careful follow-through and sensitivity to local needs and customs. And, of course, reading *The Guide to Translation and Localization*!

Donna Parrish
Publisher, *MultiLingual Computing & Technology*

Contents

Foreword iv
1. Welcome to the World of Localization 2
2. Learning the Lingo 5
3. What are My Options? 9
4. Getting Started - Obtaining an Estimate 15
5. Process is the Key to Success 22
6. Producing Native Quality Content 28
7. Engineering the Localization Process 38
8. Quality Assurance - How to be Certain You Got it Right 48
9. Formatting Print and Online Documents 53
10. Writing for Localization - Advice for Technical Writers 60
11. Same Language, Different Dialect 67
12. Writing and Displaying Asian Characters 76
13. Localization Case Studies 79
14. Single-Source Content Management 88
15. But They Speak English, Right? 96
16. Testing and Integration of Software and Hardware 100
17. Cultural Training and Awareness 106
18. Translation and Localization Today, Tomorrow, and the
    Day After 111

Translation and Localization Glossary 116
Resources 122
Contact Info 124

The Guide to Translation and Localization

Chapter 1: Welcome to the World of Localization

Scott Ludwigsen
President

One of the many great things about our team at Lingo Systems is how many cultures are represented. The founders are natives of Germany and the Netherlands, our Engineering Manager is a native of France, our Quality Assurance Supervisor is a native of Italy, our Systems Manager is a native of China, and our Operations Manager was raised in West Africa. A total of 72 languages in all! As for me, my heritage is Norwegian (plus some English, Irish, and German for good measure). Although I don't know that my roots go back to the Vikings, I do believe that new adventures are always just over the horizon.

Our entire team at Lingo Systems is very excited to bring you the fifth edition of *The Guide to Translation and Localization*. Over the last six years we have distributed more than 15,000 copies of this book in an ongoing effort to educate clients and friends about the localization process. We hope that we have had some success. Previous editions have won several national awards from the Society for Technical Communication (STC) and we are told by many that they consider it to be the definitive source of information about translation and localization.

Once again, we have designed *The Guide to Translation and Localization* to be an easy read that provides guidance on all aspects of the localization process. For our readers who are new to localization, we define key terms, explain the various options for translating materials, identify issues to consider when procuring localization services, describe the localization process itself, and provide many tips to control costs and improve quality. Localization veterans will find useful information on emerging trends, as well as technical discussions about software localization and the latest publishing techniques.

New for the fifth edition, we are excited to expand the scope of *The Guide to Translation and Localization* to include chapters from four of our strategic partners. Each of these industry leaders provides proven solutions for helping companies expand globally. We are confident that you will find their contributions to be both informative and entertaining. The services that these partners provide and the topics they address include the following:

- Single-source content management tools can often reduce the time and expense needed to create documentation and online content. AuthorIT Software Corporation not only provides an affordable, out-of-the-box solution in multiple languages, it facilitates localization and multilingual publishing. Paul Trotter's article in Chapter 14 explains single-source content management tools, how they help companies produce localization-friendly materials, and other related benefits.

Chapter 1: Welcome

- Developing a global brand that works in every language or culture is a key success factor when expanding into new markets. Brandfluency is a team of brand, localization, and print professionals who understand how to leverage a brand identity into any of over seventy languages. In Chapter 15, Perry Brooks describes how to ensure that a brand's core elements and values are not diluted or lost in translation.

- Functional testing is a key component of software localization. PCTest offers enterprise-wide testing for hardware, software, and web/e-commerce applications. Core testing solutions include compatibility, load and stress, functionality, accessibility, benchmarking, and performance. Wasi Wahedi's article in Chapter 16 describes the importance of Quality Assurance (QA) testing and the many types of tests that can be performed to ensure that a product is ready for the global marketplace.

- Organizations often must make significant cultural adjustments when entering new markets. Training Management Corporation provides cultural training and awareness through classroom, web-based, and knowledge-on-demand learning solutions in areas such as cross-cultural management, global diversity, multicultural team development, and global management and leadership. Danielle Walker's article in Chapter 17 provides a broad overview of cultural training and how it contributes to a successful global expansion.

We end with another guest chapter on the future of the localization industry from our co-publisher, MultiLingual Computing, Inc. Their unique perspective and insight makes this a *must read* for all of us who dedicate our professional lives to this important industry. MultiLingual Computing, Inc. is *the* information source for the localization, internationalization, translation, and language technology industry and we are honored to co-publish the fifth edition with them. Their publications take several forms including the printed magazine, *MultiLingual Computing & Technology*, and the biweekly e-newsletter, *MultiLingual News*. They also co-sponsor the Localization World Conference. For more information, go to **www.multilingual.com**.

As with previous editions, this book is truly a group effort. Twelve Lingo Systems employees wrote sections, and another eight provided further input, comments, questions, and stories. Moreover, rather than being written in one voice, each chapter reflects the personality of its author, allowing you to develop a feel for the diversity of cultures, talents, and experience here at Lingo Systems. Pictures of the contributors are scattered throughout the Guide to let you put a face to the names you will find in the acknowledgment section.

While we hope that you will read *The Guide to Translation and Localization* in its entirety, each chapter has been written to stand alone and be read when needed. You may find, for example, that certain chapters are relevant for your marketing staff, others for your engineering staff, and yet others for your tech pubs department. Ideally, you will find them all helpful with useful information for everyone in your organization.

Finally, we have again provided a number of translation mistakes in our "Oops" sections. These are funny stories of how some translations have gone awry. Many of the "Oops" were provided to us by linguists from around the world who have had to correct bad translations that were not performed by professionals. We expect that you will find them to be humorous...but we also want to illustrate an important point: failing to gain market share because your product seems "foreign" or "low quality" is not a laughing matter.

We hope you enjoy *The Guide to Translation and Localization* and find it a valuable tool for communicating with your multilingual customers and employees both here in the US, and throughout the world.

Sincerely,

Scott Ludwigsen
President
Lingo Systems

Chapter 2: Learning the Lingo

There is much confusion as to how the terms *globalization*, *internationalization*, *localization*, and *translation* should be used. These terms are thrown about in the press, by product developers, by marketing departments, by product management, and by the localization vendors themselves in myriad ways. Yet understanding these terms and their corresponding processes is a critical first step when considering expansion into the competitive global marketplace. You may run into people using these terms in different ways, but here is how we interpret them.

Globalization

The process of conceptualizing your product line for the global marketplace so that it can be sold anywhere in the world with only minor revision. It is most easily thought of as your global marketing strategy and is associated with all marketing concepts (branding, establishing market share, and the like). Globalization is particularly important in consumer industries such as clothing and food. Anyone, anywhere in the world can drink Coca Cola or wear Levi Strauss jeans, for example.

Internationalization

The process of engineering a product so that it can be easily and efficiently localized. Engineering can take the form of something as basic as document layout, for example, to the more complex enabling of software to handle double-byte character sets. See the sections on Engineering and Writing for Localization (Chapters 7 and 10) for more details on how to internationalize your products.

Localization

The process of customizing a product for consumers in a target market so that when they use it, they form the impression that it was designed by a native of their own country.

Translation

The process of converting the written word of a source language into the written word of a target language. Translation is a crucial component of localization.

Chapter 2: Learning the Lingo

Jeff Williams
Marketing Programs Manager

This marks the third Guidebook that I have had the pleasure to work on. I guess I could tell you that my hair was jet black before I started working on the first Guidebook, but that wouldn't be true. I was totally white by the age of 26 and people have assumed that I've been retired since then (I wish). I'm just happy to have hair!

These four terms fit together as a "bull's eye" diagram. Globalization envelops the entire concept of taking your product line global. Internationalization is performed so that the product can then be localized. Finally, translation is the *base* component of the entire process, as it represents the language transformation.

To better understand the difference between these terms, imagine that you are a product manager for a new software application that manages sales contacts. Your product development team likely assembled comments from distributors throughout the world whose customers requested new features for your yet-to-be designed contact management software. Your marketing department has determined the global demand for such a product and has developed a global branding campaign. Your design team begins work on the look and feel of the software. Here is where internationalization comes into play. You and your team must consider the following:

- Color scheme and graphic selection that avoids offending potential customers,
- Dialog boxes wide enough to accommodate text expansion,
- Functionality that supports various date, time, and currency formats,
- Input and output functionality that supports the various character sets (including double-byte characters for the Asian market),
- Right justified text fields to prevent expanded text from overlapping the graphics, and
- A readily adaptable user interface to allow British customers to read from left to right or Arabic customers to read from right to left.

Selling your contact management software to the customers in your new markets will likely require localizing the user's manual, software, help files, and user interface from English into each target language. Fortunately, proper internationalization may lower your costs. One software manufacturer found that nearly fifty percent of all support costs came from consumers in foreign markets who could not understand English documentation.

Other Key Terms

There are several other related terms that you should also be familiar with when you are ready to reach a multilingual audience.

Content Management

A software application for creating, maintaining, storing, and publishing content that makes it possible to organize and publish in multiple mediums from one central database.

Cultural Assessment

Analyzing an individual's cultural preferences through comparative analyses allows individuals to acquire the awareness and knowledge necessary for building effective skills and behavioral adaptations for multicultural management and business.

Cultural Orientation

Developing cultural self-awareness and effective behavioral strategies to minimize the cultural gaps that occur with contrasting value orientations of different social groups.

Integration Testing (Interoperability)

Confirmation that two or more systems (computers, communication devices, networks, software, and other information technology components) are able to interact with one another and exchange data according to a prescribed method in order to achieve predictable results.

International Brand Development

Giving a product the look and feel of having been developed in the target country. This requires that your brand or message be clear, easily identifiable, and culturally acceptable to the target market. A successful brand can be conveyed clearly and concisely, regardless of the language or writing source.

Chapter 2: Learning the Lingo

Tenzin Dickey
Junior Accountant

Tashi Delek! My name is Tenzin Dickey. My parents are originally from Tibet, but I was born and raised in the small town of Dharmsala, India. Independent, thoughtful, capable. A traveler. Sister to many good friends. Lover of nature and music from the soul.

Interpretation

The process of converting the spoken word of a source language into the spoken word of a target language. This is done in two main ways. The first, and most impressive to watch, is simultaneous interpretation. In this process, a person is actually *thinking* in two languages at one instant (hearing the speaker in one language and immediately converting it into the target language, and speaking that target language for others to hear). The more traditional interpretation practice is delayed interpretation where an entire thought is expressed by the speaker, the speaker pauses, and the interpreter converts the content for the target language speakers to hear. Large-scale interpretation companies now exist that have call centers with interpreters for many different languages who are available twenty-four hours a day, seven days a week for medical, legal, and business interpreting.

Multilingual Print Production

Producing packaging, advertising, and related collateral in multiple languages for simultaneous release.

Verification Testing

Confirmation of any testable requirement, including functional testing of hardware and software system components, compatibility testing of one component to another, design verification, compliance to industry standards, and third party interoperability.

Localizing your product, while sometimes challenging, pays handsome rewards. Major software and hardware manufacturers report that sixty percent or more of their business revenue is now earned outside the US. By offering your products around the world, in versions that appeal to each locale, your organization can increase its distribution, extend the shelf-life of products, and ultimately be less dependent upon the American market.

Moreover, even if you only plan to sell your products in the US, you could still be missing up to twenty percent of your potential market if your materials are just available in English. Current studies indicate that more than 45 million people in the US do not speak English - more then the entire population of Spain! Once you learn the lingo, you too can begin to reach a multilingual audience.

Chapter 3: What are My Options?

Your executive management has finally made the commitment to sell your company's products in international markets and you were just given the green light to begin localization. This is an exciting time for your organization. A whole new set of challenges and opportunities for growth lie ahead. It is worth taking on these challenges. As a bonus, what you learn along the way about globalization and localization could dramatically expand your company's markets, increasing both revenue and profits.

So how do you identify the many options available for localizing your products or materials—and how do you select the right one for your company? Your first step, after reading *The Guide to Translation and Localization*, is to define the scope of your project. To ensure that your expectations are met, accurate and realistic decisions about timeline, cost, and quality must be made prior to project start, including which of these variables are most important. Once you have a clear idea regarding what is needed, where you want to go, and when you need to arrive, you will then be in a position to talk with localization providers to see what services they offer, how much time they will take, and how much localization will cost.

During the analysis and planning stages, keep in mind that localization is a team sport. Most projects are relatively complex. They require numerous specialized resources, each functioning to provide unique and closely interrelated contributions.

The following table provides a brief summary of the different options you can choose to get your materials translated. It is not meant to be an exhaustive list of all possible alternatives, but it does cover some of the most common and obvious ways to convert written materials from one language to another. As you will see, there are many ways to get from point A to point β.

Coors' slogan, "Turn it Loose," was translated into Spanish as "Suffer From Diarrhea."

Chapter 3: What are My Options?

Overview of Translation Options

LOCALIZATION OPTIONS	CHARACTERISTICS	BENEFITS	LIMITATIONS	CONSIDERATIONS
Acquaintance or family friend	Someone you know who happens to speak or has studied the target language	Very low or no cost	• Not a localization professional • Limited capacity • No QA steps • No tools • No process • No technical expertise • Extended timelines • Consistency and quality are probably poor • High risk of missing deadlines • Hidden costs • Updates are expensive	• Being able to speak a language does not make someone a translator • You get what you pay for
Bilingual employee	Someone in your company who happens to speak the target language	• Low out-of-pocket cost • May have subject matter expertise	• Not a localization professional • Limited capacity • No QA steps • No tools • No process • Extended timelines • Consistency and quality are probably poor • High risk of missing deadlines • Hidden costs • Updates are expensive	• They have a regular, full-time job. • They might not be available when you need them. • Using in-house resources to REVIEW your vendor's final deliverable is highly recommended
Overseas distributor	• Foreign distributor, agent or representative • Translation "cost" may be negotiated as part of overall sales agreement	• Low out-of-pocket cost • May have subject matter expertise • Someone else is responsible for project	• Not a localization professional • Limited capacity • No QA steps • No tools • No process • Extended timelines • Consistency and quality may be poor • High risk of missing deadlines • Hidden costs • Updates are expensive	• Localization costs should be negotiated *up front* when the distribution agreement is prepared • You may lose control over content and quality • Ownership, copyright, and IP issues are all a concern • Unauthorized changes might be made and go undetected • Content consistency between different target languages can be difficult to maintain

Overview of Translation Options (cont.)

Localization Options	Characteristics	Benefits	Limitations	Considerations
Online machine translation	Just to get the *gist* of written text	Free, often humorous results	Free, often humorous results	Proceed with caution; you get what you pay for
Individual translator	• Independent contractor • Specializes in one language • Usually can be found locally	• Translation professional • Easy access • Quick turn around on small projects	• May not have translation memory and other sophisticated tools • Limited capacity • Longer timelines on larger projects • No independent QA (if any) • Quality may be an issue • Updates could be expensive • May have no DTP capability • One language pair only	• For small, single-language projects this might be the right solution • Expect to provide a lot of project management support for ongoing single or multiple-language translation efforts • With only one linguistic step, quality may or may not be good enough
Full-Service multiple-language vendor	An organization whose sole purpose is to provide a broad range of linguistic services	• Localization professionals • Unlimited capacity • High quality & consistency • Aggressive deadlines can be met • Multiple QA steps • Sophisticated tools, Translation Memories • Technical expertise • Updates are quick and inexpensive • Proven process • Unlimited number of languages • Project management provided • Full range of related services	• May be overkill for small one-time projects	• Use the right resources for the right job • Outsourcing localization allows you to focus on what you do best

Chapter 3: What are My Options?

Who Does the Translation?

Dan Johnson
Director of Sales and Marketing

Hi, I'm Dan. I was born on the open road. At least that is what I have been told. Forged in the crucible of friendly competition, my spirit craves acceleration. I don't mean to brag, but I have a pretty respectable power-to-weight ratio for a man of my size. The soles of my shoes are low profile to minimize weight transfer in the corners. My lap times are very consistent, and I'm easy on equipment.

Let's start with the goal in mind. How do you want to be perceived in the marketplace? Is OK good enough? If you are able to command a premium for offering the best product, can you afford to have consumers chuckle (at best) or be frustrated (at worst) over the accompanying documentation? Similarly, what is the value of being first to market with a new product? Is it worth saving a few dollars on localization but taking an extra couple of weeks to release it?

When delivering a fully localized product, it should not be apparent to the end user that the content they are reading or the product they are holding has been translated into their language from another. The fact that your product was originally created in English (for example) and then localized into the consumer's native language should be totally undetectable. A properly localized product has the look and feel of having been created specifically for the target market.

If producing well-localized products is your goal, then a few of the options listed on the previous pages can be eliminated from your consideration. In most cases, using either machine translation or non-professional resources such as family members, acquaintances or co-workers who happen to speak a given language does not produce consistently accurate, stylistically natural, or professional-quality localized content.

The use of a locally based, single-language translator can be an effective solution for small projects with one target language. This option works best when translating from English into a common language (so that it is easy to find a linguist), when the source materials have simple formatting (such as Microsoft Word), and when subsequent updates are unlikely, timelines are flexible, and projects are infrequent. As the volume of work and/or the number of target languages increases, some of the limitations will become increasingly significant. Keep in mind that the management and coordination load will increase exponentially as the number of target languages grows. Furthermore, the efficiency and cost savings gained through use of a dynamic, multi-step localization process and sophisticated localization tools (discussed later in this book) will become more and more important as well.

Chapter 3: What are My Options?

Domestic vs. Overseas

You may be tempted to use your overseas office to localize your product. They speak the language after all, so it should be easy, right? The temptation is even greater if you have an in-country subsidiary or distributor offering to do the translation for you. While it is true that these options may be the best solution in some cases, it can also lead to other problems:

- Less control from headquarters,
- Difficulty in project coordination and communication (if nothing else, the time zone will be an issue),
- Unauthorized changes to the content,
- Risks to schedule, and
- Incorrect translations (these people are not professionals).

Remember, when you send your materials to an overseas office or distributor, you create an opportunity for them to control both your content and message. The in-country team may have different priorities than your US based team, so expect to find changes to branding, use of different terminology, and perhaps features that have been disabled or removed from the US version.

Unfortunately, you might not become aware of these modifications until a problem arises or someone translates the in-country translations back to English—and you might be surprised at what you find. At Lingo Systems, we have a client who went this route and was alarmed to discover that the client's foreign office had deleted all of the contact information for tech support in the event of a problem (i.e., the phone numbers for the foreign office) and instead had substituted a comment instructing the consumer to contact the reseller with any problems!

Stories such as this can be avoided by using the right people for the right job. In most cases, the best result will be obtained by using a professional localization resource for translation, and then your own in-country representatives for terminology list development and final review of the localized content. This will enable you to coordinate the localization efforts centrally, while still involving your overseas office to encourage buy-in on the final product.

The Guide to Translation and Localization

Your final choice is whether to hire individual translators yourself or use a full-service localization vendor to manage all of your localization efforts. The issues to consider here include time, quality, budget, and the need for value-added services. Do you have the time and staff to hire and manage translators and assess the quality of their results? A full-service vendor can provide you with all the resources necessary for you to receive high quality translations on time and on budget, reducing your need to be involved in the day-to-day execution of the project.

As you consider all of the available options, keep in mind that the goals you set for your project will likely lead you toward the best solution.

"The Donghu Hotel offers Chinese and Western-style food with different flavors furnished with Banquet Hall, Western-style food Hall, Coffee House totaled 34 and 1600 seats for dinner. The celebrated kitcheners do it in person, the appetizing delicacy, tea and pastries from soup to nuts. The cuisine satisfied with various request of the honored guest and it mainly offers E dish, assembling Yue, Chuan, Hu, Zhe dishs and so on. The Hotel offers Chinese and Western-style food banquet, bender, team meal, buffet and zero service. It is good at the reception service of the slap-up feast and banquet for take charge of the reception of the national leaders in long-term. The slap-up facilities, appetite and service will take you upscale enjoyment."

Chapter 4: Getting Started - Obtaining an Estimate

As described in Chapter 3, there are several options for localizing your materials. Selecting the correct resource, however, is only the first of many issues that will need to be addressed in order to choose the best solution. Some of the *big picture* questions that should be answered before you begin are:

- What is your long-term globalization strategy?
- How do you (or should you) position your company (i.e., market leader vs. specialty supplier; top-of-the line standard setter vs. low cost alternative; custom manufacturer vs. commodity production; or high-quality provider vs. low-quality solution)?

Other, more basic considerations are also important:

- Which products and components should you localize?
- What target markets and languages do you need?
- What are the legal, regulatory, liability, and commercial requirements in the target market(s)?
- What is your timeline?
- What level of quality and consistency will you need?
- What is the likelihood and extent of on-going future updates?
- How often will you have new products for localization?
- Are there engineering and functionality issues?

With so many questions to answer, perhaps the paramount one is, "How are you going to do it?" The *Guide to Translation and Localization* has these answers and many more.

Chapter 4: Getting Started

How Much to Localize?

Ursula Mühlhaus Moyer
Co-owner

My extensive background in linguistics brought me to the translation industry a long time ago. After all these years I still continue to be fascinated and challenged by the rapid evolution of the localization industry to meet our clients' needs. I am particularly proud that the previous editions of our Guidebook have won awards, and educated our clients around the world.

The first question many companies ask is, "How many components should I localize?" The answer can be anything from "only the essentials" to "all content for all product components." The second question they ask is, "How much can I afford to localize?" When trying to answer this question, however, a better question might be, "What is the impact of not doing it?" By choosing *not* to localize certain products, you run the risk of missing out on potential sales, or even worse, offending the target consumers in a new market by not providing information in their language. Depending on the product, you could also find yourself in violation of various legal or regulatory requirements, possibly even preventing distribution of the product in the target market. In fact, at Lingo Systems, we strongly recommend that you consult with the appropriate authorities regarding the legal implications of not localizing some or all content whenever you expand into a new market.

Unfortunately, when evaluating the business case for localization, many companies only factor in how much they will spend. Do not make this mistake! An equally important question is, "How much incremental revenue can we reasonably expect to generate?" In our experience, your international sales and marketing staff will most often drive the commercial justification to localize.

Another item to consider when deciding how much to localize is whether economies of scale might be available. Once a localization program is established, it is often just as easy to translate into twenty-four languages as it is to translate into one. File preparation, project management, and back-office administration are just a few of the more obvious efficiencies to be gained.

Finally, depending on the nature of your products or services, you may not actually have much of a choice. For example, if software developers want to increase customer usability, in addition to the software application itself, you will need to consider localizing the help files, legal warranties, *read me* files, installers, user guides, and installation instructions as well. Other examples include training material developers who must decide which courses should be taught in which languages and consumer electronics manufacturers who need to evaluate the merits of supplementing user documentation with customer support websites, and other online resources.

Chapter 4: Getting Started

Fortunately, localization of virtually any component is straightforward with the right planning and the right technology. Several tools and methodologies have been developed which allow you and/or your localization partner to "recycle" translated content across many different media types. These tools include translation memory databases (discussed in Chapter 7) and single-source content management systems (discussed in Chapter 14). By reducing the volume of new text that needs to be localized, costs are reduced, timelines are shortened, and consistency is improved across all components.

Plan Early

As the old carpenter's saying goes, measure twice, cut once. In other words, it is important to plan carefully and early for localization. For example, if your documentation includes twenty screen captures from the software User Interface (UI), the UI needs to be localized *before* the documentation (or at least before the documentation is proofread so that terminology that is frozen in the UI can be propagated to the documentation and/or the help files). Even when tight timelines require that UI and documentation localization occur simultaneously, aggressive schedules can be manageable. Because these projects frequently involve the translation of thousands of words, vendors form teams of linguists to work on both components at the same time. At some point in the schedule, after the UI is frozen, time is allocated to allow the documentation to *catch up* so that references to buttons, menus, etc. in the text of the documentation match the terminology used in the UI. Fortunately, other components such as training materials and Internet content can usually wait until the bulk of the product localization is complete—after all, end users can't be trained until you have something on which to train them!

One Language at a Time or All at Once?

Many international companies prefer to roll out new products to all of their markets in a simultaneous or "sim-ship" release. Although such releases are a goal of some multinationals, they are not a commercial priority for everyone.

The Guide to Translation and Localization

Chapter 4: Getting Started

Nicole Benjamin
Account Manager

Tradition dictates a natural casing. Also needed: freshly steamed poppy-seed bun, yellow mustard, chopped onion, sweet pickle relish, tomato slices, hot sport peppers, dill pickle spear and a dusting of celery salt. Lounge comfortably in a bed of fries. This, my dear reader, is a Chicago hot dog. The mundane converts to sublime. Any questions?

A simultaneous release poses two main challenges for localization. To release English and localized products at the same time, localization generally needs to begin while the English is still under development. This means that each last-minute change to the UI, online help, or other documentation must also be incorporated by the localization team. As you can probably imagine, such stops and starts make configuration management more complicated *and* increase the cost of the project.

Given these challenges, you may want to consider an iterative development lifecycle where you provide your localization vendor with the *alpha* or *beta* version of the software. Later, when you go to *functional complete*, the vendor can finalize the translations. This approach means a little more work, but everything is finished at the same time. Alternatively, if you choose to do a delayed release, that is, localizing your components as they are needed, you can lay the groundwork with your vendor so that each component is ready to roll through the production process as soon as you give the go-ahead.

The second main challenge involves localization team complexity and resource limitations. Depending on the word count, timeline, and number of languages, your localization vendor may need to assemble teams of translators, copy editors, and proofreaders to translate the content. There may also be several teams of desktop publishers to lay out each page; two, three, four, or more quality assurance (QA) reviewers to inspect the work upon completion; and multiple localization engineers processing and preparing the files for each step. Coordinating all of this activity will be one or more project managers. At Lingo Systems, we have worked on large rollouts to thirty or more countries that required a team of more than one hundred professionals! When you look for a localization vendor, make sure they have the resources and experience to handle your project.

Getting an Estimate

You have done your homework. You have scoured the latest issues of *MultiLingual Computing and Technology* magazine. You have spoken to your counterparts in the Society for Technical Communication. You may have even checked your local telephone directory, or perhaps conducted an internet search. And, after compiling a list of potential vendors, you cannot wait to hear what they can do for you.

Chapter 4: Getting Started

As you begin your discussions, the vendors will have many questions. You will undoubtedly be asked to clearly articulate your requirements and to provide electronic source files for the vendors to analyze. This stage is all about exchanging information. What information do the vendors need? What information do you want in return? Depending on the size of your project, you may even consider following a formal Request for Information (RFI) or Request for Quote (RFQ) process. Remember, assumptions represent risk for both you and the vendors, so the more information you provide and the clearer and more concise your instructions, the more accurate the estimate and more realistic the project plan will be.

To help differentiate between vendors, many companies will ask for a sample translation as part of the bidding process. This can be a useful tool if your materials are highly technical and you want to ensure that the localization provider is qualified to handle the translations (i.e., has linguists with the appropriate subject matter expertise). A word of caution, however. If a localization provider wants to make a good impression, they will probably use their best linguist to translate your sample. Unfortunately, it does not necessarily follow that the same linguist will be available (or utilized) if the vendor is awarded the work.

Asking for references can be a fantastic way to evaluate and compare potential vendors. As with sample translations, you will almost assuredly be provided with contacts who will provide positive feedback, so your objective should be to get a feel for the style and strengths of each vendor in order to determine which one will be the best fit for your company. A good place to start is to ask for references from companies whose projects were similar in size, scope, and type to yours. Then, when speaking with the references, ask them to describe their experience working with the vendor: what was helpful, how long did the project(s) take, and how was the customer service? It is also important to learn how long the references have worked with the vendor. Reliability and long-term consistency will be very important factors in your selection.

Selecting a Vendor

Unless you provide a template with your instructions, it is likely that you will find that each localization provider has a slightly different way of presenting their estimate to you. Some vendors will respond with a great deal of information detailing the specific tasks they propose to perform, the amount of effort that is contemplated, and a business case for why they are the best choice to perform the work. Others may only submit a standard form with minimal detail.

The Guide to Translation and Localization

Chapter 4: Getting Started

Ann Chay
Business Development Manager

I live with my husband, three sons, and two very large male dogs. My life is filled with football, basketball and baseball. My grandparents migrated to Milwaukie, Oregon from Italy when they were six years of age. My family is everything you would expect of a "typical" Italian family, loud, everyone talking over everyone else, and always too much food around. This is why I feel so at home with Lingo Systems!

The process that each vendor proposes to follow on your project, the number of linguistic and QA steps to be employed, the qualification and location of the resources, and the tools that they will use will undoubtedly vary significantly. These differences can also have a huge impact on cost. But how do you choose between competing proposals when one vendor's estimate is twenty percent higher for what amounts to fifty percent more effort?

The only way to obtain the best value for your dollar is to make an *apples-to-apples* comparison, but be forewarned: this is easier said than done. In fact, standardizing estimates might be harder than herding cats. As with most things in life, you get what you pay for. Localization is no exception. Take the time to investigate each vendor's services thoroughly. Here is a starter list of questions you can use to interview a potential vendor:

- What subject matter and industry experience do you have?
- How do you qualify your linguists?
- Who would manage *my* project, where would they be located, and how would it be done?
- How often would I receive status reports on my project?
- Who would be my primary contact during the project?
- Do you use state of the art localization tools and, if so, which ones?
- When you analyze my electronic source files, do you calculate leveraging?
- How do you charge for repetitions, fuzzy matches, and unique text?
- Will you create a TM (Translation Memory database) and will I own it?
- How many projects like mine have you managed before?
- Can I speak with your customers about their experience?
- How many linguistic steps will you perform?
- What is your QA process?
- How do you develop and maintain a terminology list specific to my project?
- How do you handle changes during the course of a project?
- What is your record for delivering on time?
- Is your estimate firm or is it subject to change?

A qualified localization vendor should be able to provide an estimate that is comprehensive, accurate, and clearly defined. The table below offers a sample pricing structure covering various services and how they might be billed.

Sample Pricing Structure

PROJECT TYPE	TASK	HOW IT IS BILLED
All projects	Project management	Typically 10-15% of the project costs
	Translation, new text	Per word
	Translation, fuzzy matched text	Per word, normally less than full word rate
	Translation, 100% matched or repetitive text	Per word, normally less than full word rate
	Copy editing	Per word or per hour
	Proofreading	Per word or per hour
	Glossary/terminology development	Per term or per hour
	Translation memory creation, administration, and updating	Per hour
Documentation	Desktop publishing	Per hour or per page
	Output of film or RC paper	Per page
	PDF creation (Print or Functional)	Per hour or per page
	Quality assurance	Per hour
Software, website, & online help	Desktop publishing	Per hour or per page
	Help generation & QA	Per hour
	Screen shots, capturing & placing	Per screen shot or per hour
	Engineering	Per hour
	Functional testing	Per hour
	Graphics and screen captures	Per hour

Selecting the right localization partner can be a critical component to the overall success of your expansion into new multinational or multilingual markets. The tangible value of a long-term partnership also cannot be overemphasized. Such a relationship provides a means for the localization team to learn about your company, constituents, and products inside and out. Often this will mean improved workflows, shorter timelines, and lower costs for you. The better your partner understands you, and your product line, the more smoothly the localization process can proceed, and the more effectively project management and communication protocols can be fine-tuned. A long-term relationship between client and localization provider is, ultimately, the best way to achieve cost-effectiveness and quality work for each and every project.

Chapter 5: Process is the Key to Success

Dan Roth
Operations Manager

Localization is no joke. Two guys walk into a bear... That's a joke. A skeleton walks up to a bar, and orders a beer and a mop. See? Another joke. Let epsilon be smaller than zero. That's a math joke. I don't even know what it means. However, I do know what localization means. Read this book, then you will too. (If I was going to write a joke book, I'd give it a joke name like *Who's Who in Antarctica*.)

What is a successful localization project? For the client, it is receiving deliverables of the highest quality, on-time and on-budget (or even better, early and under budget!). For the localization provider, it is consistently producing high-quality deliverables on-time and at a profit. The similarity of goals for both parties is clear and this overlapping definition of success has created a central truth in localization: process is the key to success.

Localization used to be simple. More often than not it was a printed operator's manual or user's guide that sat on the shelf. Today, many companies realize that they can grow and increase profits by providing even greater value to their customers—wherever they may be. As such, localization likely means a simultaneous, world-wide rollout of user manuals, service manuals, online help on the company website, CD help included with the product or as part of the software, packaging materials (box art, labels, inserts, envelopes, etc.), Graphical User Interface (GUI), website updates, and more. Localization is certainly not as simple as it used to be; at least that is how it would appear at first glance. Fortunately, if you have selected the right vendor, they are going to make your localization project easy for you because they are going to follow a proven, effective, and efficient process that yields consistent, high-quality deliverables.

Before going much further, it is important to note that not all processes are created equal. For example, vendors can vary the number of linguistic steps they use when translating your work. Some employ a single step, some two, and others, three. Some vendors hire a vendor to sub-contract the linguistic work (and may not bother to qualify the resources), others partner with and form long-term relationships with in-country language providers, while still others employ on-site linguists. Quality assurance reviews may be non-existent, minimal, or in-depth (with regression checking included). Desktop publishing may be performed by the project manager or by trained formatters. As with the source materials themselves, localization processes can be very complex, involving many disciplines (translation, copy editing, proofreading, engineering, desktop publishing, quality assurance, and in-country review). The need to effectively coordinate and execute these tasks is the reason that the right process is so key.

A good vendor will have a process that forms the backbone for all their projects. The process will be the same regardless of the type of project or file: documentation, software, or help. A good process promotes cost effectiveness, consistency, quality, and flexibility. Costs are controlled, because each member of the team is clear on the tasks they need to complete and the timeframe allotted to do so. Consistency is achieved, because assigned tasks are executed to the required standards the same way each time. And perhaps most importantly, by having a documented plan, there is always a reliable starting point for problem solving and adapting to varying project requirements.

At this point, you may be asking yourself, "Why should I be interested in the process used by my vendor? My only concerns are that my vendor delivers my translated files on time and under budget." For this to happen, however, a lot must go on between the time when you hand over your files to your vendor and when you receive your delivery. It is important you understand the process followed between these two dates because it is this process that will ensure your website is in French on the day all of your new French customers type your URL into their browsers.

Communication

Communication is the cornerstone of successful project management in any field, and it is at the core of a good localization process as well. The project manager (PM) must effectively communicate your needs to the translation and localization team working on your project, and similarly communicate issues they identify back to you and your colleagues.

Typically, representatives from both sides (the client and the provider) work together throughout the project, with the localization PM serving as the main conduit of communication. Most often, the client side is made up of a key contact person, an in-country reviewer provided by the client (often someone from the target country) who can offer advice on the terminology and style for your target countries, and a technical expert who can answer questions. On the localization provider side, the PM coordinates directly with all project resources, including software engineers, desktop publishers, quality assurance specialists, and linguists. Any issues raised by the localization team are funneled back to the client by the PM for resolution.

Chapter 5: Process is Key

It is important to clearly communicate your expected delivery dates, delivery format, and media at the beginning of the project. Similarly, your localization team should confirm their understanding of your requirements back to you to ensure that everyone is on the same page. On many projects, the localization provider determines the timeline at the project start based upon your specifications and the availability of linguistic and technical resources. The PM should also confirm the anticipated delivery date with you so that all expectations are met.

Remember, you know your product better than anyone else. Your localization vendor will appreciate receiving as much information as possible before your project starts (such as previous glossaries, terminology lists, or product descriptions).

Your localization project manager should work with you to formulate clear expectations for what the lines of communication will be. This allows all questions or issues that arise during the project to be dealt with in an effective and timely manner. In the event that you are away from your office while your document is being localized, always bring your replacement up to speed on the project's progress and be sure to let your PM know whom to contact with questions while you are away.

Beyond the fruitful transfer of information between you and your PM, clearly defined status reports should be given to you by your localization provider. Status reports can be as informal as an email, or as formal as a posted report via a user interface on a website. The point is that you can, and should, request summary reports that meet your specific needs.

On a sign in a small French harbor town in Brittany: "The dumping of dead bodies is strictly prohibited."

Chapter 5: Process is Key

During the Project

The PM assigned by your localization vendor coordinates and schedules all the necessary project resources, monitors progress, trouble-shoots issues, and provides necessary information for all personnel to successfully complete the project on time. In addition, the PM should keep you informed of the status of your project based on your requested method and frequency.

Outside of these status reports, you may not hear a lot from your localization provider. Do not be alarmed by this! Rest assured that the localization team is hard at work and quite busy completing your project. Once you have turned over final files, a localization engineer begins by preparing them for translation and sending them out to the linguistic team.

A quality translation process should involve three distinct linguistic steps: translation, copy editing, and proofreading. Depending on your word count, this could take as little as a couple of days or as much as several months. Note that some providers may try to combine the translation and copy editing phases into a single step. This can reduce costs and timeline but it does so at a distinct risk to quality and consistency. Be sure you know how many steps your selected provider will perform and be certain to document it in your contract or work order.

Once the translation work is completed, your localization team will send your files through various desktop publishing, engineering, and quality assurance stages. The number of people and the type of work that happens on your files is all predicated on the type of materials being localized. A small marketing flyer into a single language probably would require a six person team: three separate linguists for translation, copy editing, and proofreading, a single desktop publisher, a quality assurance person, and the PM. Alternatively, a large operator's manual into multiple languages would have a much larger and complex team. Depending on the word count, timeline, and number of languages, your localization vendor may assemble a team of more than one hundred professionals! What is important to note is that regardless of the type of project or the size of the team, an established, effective, formalized process must always be followed to ensure good communication, quality, and consistency.

Chapter 5: Process is Key

Steve Heikkila
Project Manager

I received my Ph.D. in 1996 and worked for several years as a philosophy professor before joining Lingo in 2000. As a Kantian, I'll forego biographical information about my irrelevant empirical self and focus exclusively on the *noumenal*. As a child I was ruled by guardians because my faculty of judgment was too underdeveloped for autonomy. At 18, I cast off this tutelage and became a legislating member of a kingdom of ends. At 34, I finally understood the metaphysics of freedom without antinomy by recognizing that while freedom is the *ratio essendi* of the moral law, the moral law is the *ratio cognoscendi* of freedom.

A good process can also mitigate the disruption if you need to change or modify the source document after the project has already started. However, there are several important issues to keep in mind. Frequent changes during the course of a project can become expensive, and severely impact the original timeline. Communicate clearly what, where, and when these changes are to be made so that your PM can quickly incorporate them into the final product. Changes to the original project scope may cause an increase in localization costs and/or a delay in delivery. Your localization provider should submit an estimate for each new change, subject to your approval, that addresses both additional costs and any delivery date adjustments that may be necessary prior to incorporating the changes.

Completing the Project

For many projects, before any final files are delivered there is an in-country review (ICR) step. This is an opportunity for one of your colleagues or business partners in the target country to review the localized files and provide expert feedback and input to your vendor. This review accomplishes several things: prior to release, it puts the files in front of an expert with first-hand knowledge of the material; it creates an opportunity to gain buy-in from your international partners; and it can give you an added sense of confidence in the quality of your vendor's work. You can read more about the ICR steps and process in Chapter 6.

Once the final versions of your project are completed, they are delivered to you by the localization provider. Typically, delivery is performed electronically (either via FTP or email), though special delivery requirements could include CD-ROM, print film, or other format. You should always review your delivery to ensure that your provider addressed all your needs while performing the localization.

Feedback to the localization provider is an important final step in the project. By communicating to your provider the positive and negative experiences throughout the life of the project, process improvements can be made that will help your localization vendor provide more effective services to you and to other clients in the future. Your localization provider should solicit your comments and feedback in a standardized manner. Offer a candid critique of areas where your vendor failed to meet your expectations and praise for tasks well done.

Chapter 5: Process is Key

By now it is pretty clear why process is so important. A lot of time, money, and resources go into a localization project, so you do not want to reinvent the wheel with each new release. An established process ensures that none of your effort is wasted. This may be your first localization project, or your first time working with a new vendor. By using a well-documented and proven process, however, your localization provider is more likely to have the framework and controls in place to ensure a positive experience for you. Process really is key to making sure you receive the highest quality localization service.

From Josephine Bacon: "Several years ago, I was faxed a text from an agency in British Columbia, Canada. It was a set of phrases that the police could use to hand to motorists they had stopped who did not speak English. Those I was sent were in Hebrew, but the Hebrew was terrible. Of the horrors contained in the translation, one in particular stood out. The question from the police was supposed to be 'Are you carrying a weapon.' The word for weapon in Hebrew is the masculine 'neshek.' However, the translator had made it a feminine word by adding an 'a' - neshika. This turned the meaning of the phrase in Hebrew into 'Can I give you a kiss?'. Neshika means a kiss!"

Chapter 6: Producing Native Quality Content

Barb Weiss
Senior Project Manager

Discovered under a damp sponge in a Petri dish, Ms. Weiss quickly grew to guppy stature. Her early years went swimmingly under the care and feeding of two Senior Scientists at I. M. KLONED Laboratories. With the emergence of a dorsal fin, Ms. Weiss joined the German circus circuit performing as a transpecied fishwoman. Her German/English linguistic abilities led her to a localization career with Lingo Systems. She currently works out of a large fish tank as a localization project manager.

"Quality is job one." No doubt you have heard that before, but even though the phrase may be little more than a tired marketing message it still holds true. If you are investing hundreds or possibly thousands of dollars to translate your materials, you will undoubtedly want the highest quality available for your investment. So just what does quality mean to your localization project? How do you identify quality and how do you make sure that you are getting it? What follows is a discussion on how to enhance the linguistic quality of your localization project.

The quality of the final localized deliverable is largely dependent upon the quality of the original source text. A poorly written document in English will probably appear as a poorly written document in French as well. There is much more to consider than just grammar, however. To ensure that your source text will be localization-ready, your technical writer(s) should be informed well in advance that the documentation will be translated. It can be beneficial to put your technical writer(s) in contact with your localization vendor to ensure that the subsequent documentation is designed for a global audience. This allows cultural and other country-specific issues to be addressed early in the project, which, in turn, makes the translation process that much more effective and efficient.

There are also many tools, techniques, and procedures that can be used by your localization vendor to maximize linguistic quality. These include:

* Style guidelines,
* A glossary in the source language,
* A terminology list in the target language,
* Selection of linguists,
* Use of a three-step translation process, and
* In-country review.

Chapter 6: Linguistic Quality

Style Guidelines

Style guidelines are a list of specific rules the linguist must follow during the translation process. These guidelines are either provided by the client or are developed by the linguist in conjunction with the client. Guidelines typically address the following issues:

- Tone (formal vs. conversational) of the localized documentation,
- List of terms that should be translated, and those that should not,
- Rules for capitalization and accent marks,
- Translation of titles and subtitles,
- Conversion of measurements,
- Rules for spelling numbers,
- Use of abbreviations, and
- Punctuation rules.

Style guidelines should be developed based upon consensus of all interested parties, including the client, in-country evaluator(s), and the localization vendor. Style guidelines help to create documents appropriate for the end-user, for meeting company and country standards, and for maintaining geographic and cultural suitability.

Glossary

A glossary is a list of words and definitions that explain difficult, technical, product-specific, or industry-specific terms. Typically, the list is prepared at the start of a project by technical writers or software engineers to help guide the linguist in choosing the best translation for each of the specialized terms. In most cases, the definitions themselves are not translated unless they appear in the original document. Once client representatives have approved the list of translated glossary terms, it then forms the basis of a terminology list.

The Guide to Translation and Localization

Chapter 6: Linguistic Quality

Terminology List

Leah Carter
Accounting Manager

Comedian Steven Wright once said, "When I have a kid, I wanna put him in one of those strollers for twins, then run around the mall looking frantic." Not funny. And I can appreciate funny. I was married at an NBA game during halftime. I'm an accountant, and have recently added to my growing family. I can tell you, without a shadow of a doubt, math is easy—twins are hard.

A terminology list consists of the most important terms in the original source materials. Typically, these terms are based upon:

- The product-specific glossary developed by the technical writer of the source document,
- The already localized user interface terminology of major software developers (e.g. Microsoft),
- Software and documentation that the client may have previously localized,
- Other localized resource materials such as marketing collateral and product lists,
- Company standards (such as part numbers, technical and product support information, warranties, license agreements, copyrights, references to other software programs, product names, brand names, and non-translated terms), and
- Country standards for expressing functional or cultural dictates (such as publishing standards, sorting of lists, abbreviations, time, dates, holidays, currency, and measurements).

To develop a terminology list, a translator will closely review all source materials and extract the key terms. After gathering appropriate resources and consulting with, as needed, product developers to obtain explanations of any ambiguous terms (this may be facilitated by your localization vendor's project manager) the linguist translates the list into the target language. The translated terminology list is then systematically updated and validated throughout the localization process. Other options for developing a terminology list include having company engineers, company tech writers, or your localization vendor's project managers compile the list. The list can then be distributed to target language linguists for translation.

Obtaining sign-off from your in-country representatives before moving on is the best way to ensure that you, your vendor, and your vendor's linguists are in full agreement regarding the terms and translations on the list. Once approved, the terminology list is used by each of the linguists during the translation phase. If any additions, deletions, or modifications to the terminology list are suggested, those changes are funneled back to the lead linguist, and when necessary, to your company's engineers, tech writers, or in-country representatives, for verification.

Chapter 6: Linguistic Quality

Deciding not to develop a terminology list can be risky. There are countless examples in which one term can be accurately translated in several different ways. For example, certain terms can vary depending on whether they refer to software or hardware, or whether they are being presented in a formal, informal, or imperative context. Some terms are impossible to translate, or may need to be referred to by an abbreviation based on either the English term or the translated term. All of these issues must be resolved by the client, the vendor, and the vendor's lead linguist before the project begins.

An approved terminology list will improve linguistic quality by ensuring:

- The translator, copy editor, and proofreader all use the same, industry-specific, terminology throughout the project and over all project components,
- Consistency of abbreviations, product names, non-translated terms, and measurements,
- Consistency between country and company standards,
- Local (i.e., in-country) suitability, and
- Consensus among client, distributor, and localization provider.

Examples in Spanish

Agreement on terminology

"Congratulations" can be translated correctly into *Felicitaciones* or *Enhorabuena*.

Local suitability

"Congratulations!" as well as "Welcome to" ..... is frequently used in user manuals to introduce a new product. Should the Spanish audience be addressed in this rather colloquial American way? Is there a more formal way to address the user, or should this greeting not be used at all?

Abbreviation

UK — Reino Unido (United Kingdom)

In all cases the abbreviation is written first, with the name for which it stands written in parentheses. However, there appears to be no set standard on the placement of the translated text. Client and localization vendor need to agree if the translated text should be placed immediately after the abbreviation or after the name for which it stands.

The Guide to Translation and Localization

Chapter 6: Linguistic Quality

Examples in Japanese

Depending on the platform, commands and buttons are translated differently:

Save As	別名保存	名前を付けて保存
Cut	切り取り	カット
Print	印刷	プリント

Depending on the context, an English word can be translated into multiple terms in the target language:

Address	アドレス、 住所
Title	題名、 タイトル、 呼称
Class	クラス、 級、 レベル
Time	時間、 タイム

On the other hand, sometimes multiple terms in English can be translated into a single term in Japanese:

Tall	高い
High	高い
Expensive	高い
Pretentious	高い

Some words and abbreviations, by convention, stay in English:

lpi	**lines per inch**
pts	**points**
m/cm/mm	**meter/centimeter/millimeter**
g/kg/mg	**gram/kilogram/milligram**

A sign in the Czech Republic: "Take one of our horse-driven city tours. We guarantee no miscarriages."

The Guide to Translation and Localization

Chapter 6: Linguistic Quality

Examples in German

Variation between software and hardware technology

Setup is translated into *Einrichten* if the term refers to setting up the software and *Anschließen* if the term refers to setting up a peripheral device.

Non-translated term

In projects where the documentation is translated but the user interface stays in English, there should be an agreement about whether the English term is followed by the localized term in parentheses or vice-versa.

Klicken Sie auf Load/Unload Panel (*Stück laden/Entfernen*), or

Klicken Sie auf Stück laden/Entfernen (Load/Unload Panel)

Style

Connect your printer to the computer can be tranlated formally into:

Schließen Sie den Drucker an den Computer an.

Or in the imperative voice:

Drucker an den Computer anschließen.

Or in the passive voice:

Der Drucker muss an den Computer angeschlossen werden.

Linguist Selection

A very important key to achieving superior linguistic quality is knowing how to choose an expert linguist. On an abstract level, most people understand intuitively that a professional linguist will produce a higher quality translation than an employee who happens to speak the language or part-time college students trying to earn extra money on the side. They also understand that, as with all professions, not all linguists have equal skills or subject matter expertise. This intuitive grasp of the matter notwithstanding, however, the allure of possibly saving a few dollars is hard to ignore. Time and again, a native Japanese or Spanish speaking software engineer who worked on the development of the software is tasked with translating the UI and then the help files for a project. When this happens, a red flag should immediately pop up in your mind: are you using the right person for

Chapter 6: Linguistic Quality

Peter Kavanagh
DTP Specialist/Japanese Linguist

I have two sets of names. My Japanese name is Nao Okura. I have always preferred the name Peter. Growing up in Japan, one of the games kids played at my kindergarten was spelling out our names, and reading them backward. It turned out my Japanese name backwards is very embarassing. I don't use that name anymore.

the job? In developing the English source you probably used professional technical writers and user interface specialists to ensure that the English content was correct and appropriate for the end user. For precisely the same reasons it also makes sense to hire professional linguists to translate these materials. Engineers should do what they do best: design software, bridges, cars, and staplers. Most engineers are *not* technical writers. So, if you would never consider asking your software engineer to write your English user guide, why would you want to use a software engineer as a translator? Translators are highly trained professionals who know how to get your message across clearly and correctly so that your end users can easily understand the information.

As defined in Chapter 2, localization involves much more than word-for-word translation. Because different cultures use different grammar and sentence structures, straight word-for-word translations often do not reflect proper linguistic style or accurately capture complex concepts. Sometimes they no longer even convey the original meaning of the message. An experienced linguist, however, can accurately translate the most difficult materials and also convey nuances, ideas, and register (tone, style, formality, complexity, etc.).

Localization quality is directly linked to the translator's experience with the topic, and knowledge of both the source and target languages. The translators working on your project should provide native-quality work. Native quality means that the material, once translated, reads as though it was originally written in the target language. This usually requires the expertise of someone raised and educated in the target country. Of course, there are non-native translators with exceptional education, training, and experience in a specific language who are able to provide native-quality work, but that takes true talent.

So just what makes a good translator? A professional linguist will possess:

- Native fluency in the source language,
- A thorough understanding of the target language,
- Excellent writing skills, including a grammatical mastery of the target language and knowledge of various written forms and styles,
- Familiarity with current terminology in the desired field (experienced translators maintain extensive reference libraries),
- A working knowledge of the localization process,
- Access to appropriate tools such as up-to-date computers, multiple software applications, and industry-specific software tools such as TRADOS, and
- An acute awareness of cultural differences and language subtleties.

Chapter 6: Linguistic Quality

To obtain the highest quality translations, your localization vendor should have well-documented linguist qualification procedures (and follow them!) for evaluating and hiring individual linguists or translation agencies. The linguists they use for your projects should both be experienced translators *and* be familiar with your content subject matter. There are various ways to assess competency, and no single way is necessarily the right way. However, to ensure quality it is imperative that your localization vendor has a means to verify that only qualified professionals, with appropriate subject matter expertise are working on your project.

At Lingo Systems, we believe that a translator should meet the following clearly defined minimum criteria:

- A Bachelor's or Master's degree in an appropriate field,
- Five years of general translation experience,
- Three years of translation experience with material similar to the source material,
- Translation certifications such as those provided by the American Translators Association, and
- A demonstrated commitment to the profession through professional affiliations.

The quality of your final deliverable depends on the professional abilities of many individuals at every phase of your project's development: software/help file engineering, linguistic quality assurance, desktop publishing, etc. Keep in mind that each one of these discrete tasks requires individuals who are localization professionals. Using qualified translators will infuse your products with a professional style and clarity of content that contributes to the success of your international release.

A sign in a Bucharest office building: "The lift is being fixed for the next day. During that time we regret that you will be unbearable."

A Three-Step Translation Process

Maja Bailey
Project Manager

Remember those lines from "Pulp Fiction"? "But you know what the funniest thing about Europe is? It's the little differences. A lotta the same stuff we got here, they got there, but they're a little different." I never thought I would end up working for a localization company in the States, trying to help educate our customers about the importance of those "little differences." I was born and raised in Lidzbark Warminski, a small yet beautiful historic town in the north of Poland. I've always had a knack for languages, and graduated in German studies. Localization turned out to be a natural fit for me. If you think English is tough, try saying this one fast: Chrzaszcz brzmi w trzcinie w Szczebrzeszynie.

Many vendors use only one or two linguistic steps to localize source materials. At a minimum, a basic translation step is always performed. A second copy edit step, hopefully by a second linguist, is often employed as well. To provide the highest quality, however, a three-step process, with a different linguist performing each step, is the best way to ensure an accurate translation. A three-step process utilizes a separate:

- Translator
- Copy editor
- Proofreader

The translator is the lead linguist on your project and is responsible for converting the source material content into the target language. The copy editor then reviews, word for word, the translator's work, verifying the accuracy of the translation, including double checking the lead translator's work against the glossary, terminology list, or style guidelines that were developed at project start. Finally, the proofreader examines the final version on a stand-alone basis for consistency, proper format, and flow of the language.

While most commercial products should use a three-step linguistic process, there are cases where this is overkill. If you simply need to have your content understood in the target language, you may be able to use translation only, or translation followed by either copy editing or proofreading. A two-step approach is particularly useful for internal documents (e.g., training materials, internal memos, etc.).

Your vendor should be flexible in developing a translation team that works best for your budget, timeline, and quality requirements. For example, you may have a 40,000 word job requiring a three-step process, but delivery is a mere three weeks away. The average number of words a linguist can translate in a week is 10,000, so clearly a vendor would not be able to meet your deadline with only one translator on the project. In this scenario, your vendor may have a team of three or four translators working on different sections of the project, two or more copy editors, and one proofreader who, in addition to ensuring consistency of terminology, would also make sure that all translated material reads as one voice. In this case, given a large number of words and a short timeline, you can see that the development of a glossary, a terminology list, and a style guide would go a long way toward providing a high quality deliverable!

Chapter 6: Linguistic Quality

There are many possible linguistic team configurations that your vendor can use to successfully deliver a quality product. Sometimes, as mentioned above, a team of translators, multiple copy editors, and one proofreader makes the most sense. On another project a single translator, in conjunction with multiple copy editors and proofreaders works best. In a different scenario your vendor might use multiple translators and then have them copy edit one another's work before sending the content on to the proofreader. The key to quality when multiple linguists are working on your project is that your vendor has a plan to ensure that the final product reads as one voice, and that terminology is applied consistently. Usually that means that one linguist on the team, whether translator, copy editor, or proofreader, will review the content of the entire project.

The bottom line is that flexibility and a little creativity, along with careful preparation, will serve you well on virtually any project no matter how big the word count and how tight the deadline.

In-Country Review

The final procedure that should be employed to maximize quality is to build an in-country review into your project schedule. Checking the quality of your vendor's work by using your own in-country representatives (employees, distributors, customers, or agents) to review the translation is an excellent way for you to be sure that all materials were consistently translated—and that your message has been accurately reflected. Whomever you select, the best results will be obtained if the reviewer is familiar with your products. These reviewers can then evaluate the specifications of your product against the cultural/linguistic elements of the relevant country. If possible, in-country reviewers should be involved early in the project (at the glossary development stage), so that they are aware of all the terminology choices. Bringing an in-country reviewer on board at the project's start avoids costly rewording due to mere stylistic differences in the translation later in the game.

The Guide to Translation and Localization

Cédric Vezinet
Engineering Manager

I don't know if you have ever tried it, but having 6 weeks of vacation a year, working 35 hours a week, and having 11 public holidays gets old after a while. So, I decided to move to the US, and work 50 hours a week. It just made more sense at the time. What was I thinking!!! Well, it's kind of too late now. The US is so fond of French people that they won't even let me go back to France. So I am stuck here. I watch TV and eat Freedom Fries all day.

Chapter 7: Engineering the Localization Process

Roles of the Engineering Group

True localization is a multi-discipline activity that includes linguistics, formatting, engineering, and quality control. Engineering is an integral component of this process and is one of the services offered by a localization provider that differentiates simple translation from comprehensive localization.

Localization engineers are involved at every stage of the localization process. Often they consult on internationalization matters before the source materials are even developed. Once source files are created, the engineer's analysis of them provides vital information for planning and estimation. Linguists rely on engineers to extract text strings from source content and prepare RTF (Rich Text Format) files to facilitate translation. They also manage the ensuing translation memory and use tools such as TRADOS and Multilizer to improve consistency and lower costs. As projects wind down, engineers may perform the functional testing of the localized products.

At Lingo Systems, members of our engineering group closely interact with the other production departments to provide support. For our desktop publishing (DTP) group, they import and export text from desktop publishing applications. For our quality assurance (QA) department, they perform functional testing of technical projects such as user interfaces, websites, and help systems. And they are always available for a quick game of pool over lunch!

First Things First: Internationalization

Many companies develop their products with only a US customer in mind. When these domestic products are slated for distribution to foreign markets, the process of localization often reveals limitations in the product design. Internationalization is the process of engineering a product so that it can be localized for export to any country.

Chapter 7: Engineering

Often, internationalization is quite simple. For example, some languages use more characters and take up more space than others. A properly internationalized source file will leave room for text expansion. Another common internationalization step is to resize an 8 1/2" x 11" document to European A4 paper size.

In addition to considering overall design and layout, the internationalization process focuses on, but is not limited to, the following points:

- Does the design account for cultural differences in various metrics such as currency, units of measure, date format, phone numbers, and addresses?
- Are all the localizable strings isolated from variables and other code for easy extraction?
- Is the product free of embedded and concatenated strings?
- Is the interface designed for dynamic layout so that it can accommodate text expansion?
- Do automated lists take into account any sorting order differences in the target locale?

A sure way to avoid internationalization surprises is to involve your localization provider during the product design stage so that localization requirements can be taken into consideration during development. If this is not done, your localization vendor will likely have to perform some product internationalization prior to beginning localization, which not only may compromise timelines, but may also have an adverse effect on your budget.

Encoding: Pick your Poison

A major question to address when you begin the internationalization process is whether your application can or will use Unicode as its encoding format. Before Unicode was invented, there were dozens of different encoding systems. No single one could contain enough characters to represent every possible language. For example, the European Union alone required several different encodings just to cover its languages. Even for a single language like English no single encoding was adequate for all the letters, punctuation, and technical symbols in common use.

The Guide to Translation and Localization

Chapter 7: Engineering

Donald Arney
Project Manager

1979 Competition GS, near original. Heron headbadge. Black paint. Forks/stays are half-chromed. Gold pinstriping around lugs. Reynolds 531 double-butted tubing throughout. Campagnolo eyeletted dropouts; rears are adjustable long horizontals. Campy Gran Sport throughout. Original Weinmann 605 brakes available. Rims are 700c Weinmanns. Saddle by Brooks. Stem is marked Raleigh. "C'mon, Connie...we're in the big time, we've made it. We're not hitchhiking anymore, we're riding!"

To add to the challenge, many of these encoding systems also conflict with one another. That is, two encodings will use the same numeric assignment for two different characters, or use different numeric assignments for the same character. Computers (especially servers) must be able to support many different encodings—but it still may not be enough. Whenever data is passed between different encodings or platforms, it runs the risk of being corrupted.

Unicode eliminates most of these problems. It is well-established, works on all platforms, and supports many more characters than most of us have ever heard of or will ever use. Unicode provides a unique number for every character, no matter what the platform, no matter what the program, no matter what the language. It also allows data to be transported between many different systems without corruption. Due to the natural progression of technology, there are many different Unicode formats: UTF-7, UTF-8, UTF-16, UTF-32, and on into the future. In general, UTF-8 will be most common on the Internet. UTF16, UTF16LE, UTF16BE are used by Java and Windows. UTF32, UTF32LE, UTF32BE are used by various UNIX systems. Fortunately, the conversions between all of them are algorithmically based, and quick to implement.

Pick Early, Test Often

Many internationalization issues can be identified early in the development process by performing internationalization testing of the source material. Machine Translation (MT) technology is often used for this purpose since it can generate pseudo-translated content that has the look and characteristics of translated material without a costly investment in translation. Machine translation is based on advanced computational linguistic analysis, and because it is inexpensive, can quickly generate lots of translated content for testing purposes. Such testing can help pinpoint issues in the localization project before they become major headaches. For instance, a pseudo-translation can identify variables in the software that should not be translated, allowing you to isolate them prior to actual linguistic work.

It is important to note that MT has many drawbacks when it comes to actual translation (e.g., it requires use of constrained vocabulary, it may not convey complex or abstract concepts, etc.), but it is a very valuable tool in the internationalization phase.

Chapter 7: Engineering

Internationalization is not a service commonly offered by localization companies as it requires highly skilled and specialized personnel with a very strong understanding of the platforms and development environments being used. Moreover, a well-executed internationalization review will not necessarily rid your files of all potential localization headaches—but it will reduce them to a manageable level, and avoid the introduction of additional defects during the localization process.

In general, the difference between a successful project and one plagued by problems is a direct function of the amount of interaction between the client and vendor engineering departments in the early stages of the project. Internationalization evaluation and testing is a very cost-effective way to ensure that your product is ready for localization—especially when measured against the delays and costs associated with trying to resolve these issues during the localization process.

On Our Way: Localization Begins

Once all internationalization issues have been addressed, the localization process can begin on a good foundation. For the engineering group, this usually means preparing the source files for translation. How this is done varies depending on the type of materials. The four main categories are: documentation localization, help localization, UI localization, and Internet localization.

Page by Page: Documentation

Want to see us pull a rabbit out of our hat? Well, perhaps that's a stretch, but this is where the magic starts. Imagine you have just purchased the latest and greatest Widget. The first thing you do is read the manual, right? (C'mon, work with us here.) Now, imagine lifting all the English out of that manual, crunching it all up and then carefully unfolding it to reveal a brand new language. It's a bit of strange notion, but that's pretty much how document localization works. In simplest terms, documentation engineering is the process of importing and exporting text from a desktop publishing application.

The Guide to Translation and Localization

Since most translators work within Microsoft Word using Computer-Aided Translation (CAT) software, the source material (which can be in any medium) must be converted to an RTF file that preserves the formatting of the original document in order for the linguist to be able to work. This is done by using different tagged text formats (codes) to isolate the formatting from the translatable text. By protecting the formatting, the translators can then use their CAT tools and focus exclusively on what needs to be translated without being confused by formatting codes, which can be very numerous (especially in the case of Quark documentation).

The vast majority of documentation is developed using QuarkXPress, Adobe InDesign, Adobe PageMaker, and Adobe FrameMaker. As you can see, Adobe Systems Inc. has quite a few different writing tools, but as time goes by, they seem to be moving toward one versatile application that will address all documentation development needs. In January 2004, Adobe began transitioning its PageMaker users to InDesign. If InDesign continues to gain popularity in the technical writing community, it will make the localization process much easier. InDesign is a terrific application for localization. It offers full Unicode support, and is well-suited for cross-platform work. It also allows for XML integration with Content Management Systems.

Regardless of the application used to develop the materials, when the RTFs come back from translation they head straight to engineering. With a wave of a wand and some feverish keyboard tapping, engineers pour the localized text back into the source documents and hand them off to the desktop publishing department where they are polished to perfection.

Stop the Presses: Help File Localization

As a means of disseminating information, print documentation is quickly losing ground to interactive help systems. Well-structured online help provides users with incredible search capability, allowing them to find more information in less time than with conventional print documentation. Many help users say this leads to a richer experience. We could not agree more. Help systems are not only getting bigger, they are getting smarter. Perhaps most importantly, however, they are becoming easier and less costly (if not downright cheap) to create. Single-source publishing tools such as AuthorIT, ArborText, WebWorks, or RoboHelp are now able to import previously generated Word or FrameMaker documents and then leverage them to create interactive help systems. As more companies discover these benefits, this trend will only accelerate.

Chapter 7: Engineering

The main help formats we see being used are WinHelp, HTML Help, WebHelp, JavaHelp, Oracle Help, and the relatively new FlashHelp. Even though all these formats have their own specific uses, when it comes to localizing help systems, the approach is similar.

Interface This: Software Localization

An engineering group really shines during the localization of software. We take on all comers: Windows, Mac OS, UNIX, Linux, Palm OS, mainframe, and Java based applications. And we will take any flavor: web-based, server-based, or client-based.

For some programming language and platform combinations, software localization requires a process not unlike the one used for documentation. The localization engineer extracts the text from the application and then creates a tagged RTF file for the translator that protects the underlying codes. In other cases, the localization engineer uses a proprietary tool or off-the-shelf application like Catalyst or Multilizer that allows the translator to work directly on compiled files and executables. All things being equal, however, it is more common and easier to work in the resource (RC) files or properties files to minimize the amount of preparation work and reduce the potential for defects being introduced during the localization process.

Whatever method is used, one thing is sure: the continuing evolution of Unicode technology and the greater understanding of the needs of the international market has made localization engineering much easier. The latest OS editions from Microsoft and Apple are perfect illustrations.

The combination of Windows XP and Office XP (a.k.a. Office 2003) is a must-have when dealing with multiple languages in your day-to-day operations. It is now possible to easily generate text files in many encodings for the most widely used languages on any Western operating system. The manipulation of Eastern languages, double-byte, and even right-to-left languages has been made much easier, too. We used to have to navigate from one native operating system to the next just to manipulate localized files. Much of this tussle has now disappeared and native operating systems are only used for online functional testing of the final localized product.

Also widely used and indispensable is Apple and its Mac operating system. OS X, and especially its latest Panther release, is not only a great system for localization but, in our opinion, the most localization-friendly operating system on the market. With just a simple drag of the mouse, users are able to switch the UI and/or the system's language.

Chapter 7: Engineering

Chris van Grunsven
Senior Localization Engineer

In the beginning there was...me! I have been with Lingo Systems since it started in 1992. That is not to say that I am the omniscient guru of all-that-is localization; I am still learning and hope to never stop. If you want to talk localization or early ('66-'67) Broncos, look me up.

No matter what the platform, the best way to make your UI localization-friendly is to externalize all localizable strings (similar to Java's properties file). Whenever possible, design your UI so that most of the strings are located in well-formatted files where the variables are followed by the string and the interface is dynamically laid out. Another important rule is to avoid string concatenation.

Going World Wide: Web Localization

User Interfaces are increasingly web-based because they are easier to maintain and offer more support than client-based applications. In most cases, both web-based applications and commercial websites have a database such as Oracle, SQL Server, MySQL, or Access as the back end. Fortunately, no matter what the type of database, the same process and tools (e.g. Multilizer) are used for localization.

From an engineering perspective, the most important step in localizing a database is to have well-defined requirement spec sheets listing the tables and the fields requiring localization. It also helps to have the database designed in such a way as to facilitate either field or table localization. From there, the only other hurdle could be string length limitations, but these are easily managed with tools such as Multilizer.

As with many things in life, however, what is good for the goose may not be as good for the gander. Websites that have been built with dynamic content are usually very localization friendly for engineers. In most cases, it is relatively easy for us to extract the text strings from the underlying database. Unfortunately, once the text has been extracted, it is not so friendly for the linguists who have to translate the strings.

Rather than working with a complete document, all the translator gets to see are random, out-of-context strings; a difficult challenge for even the most skilled professional. It is, therefore, a good idea to use a description field in your database to give some guidance to the linguists. With proper instructions, the engineer will be able to include non-translatable fields in the translation packages that are provided to the translator.

The most compelling advantage of a database-backed website is the downstream benefit. Updates (including localization maintenance) become very easy and very inexpensive. As changes are made to the site, the new and modified strings are extracted, translated, and then reinserted. In many cases, localization delivery can even be automated using third-party tools.

Chapter 7: Engineering

There can be other challenges to localizing a website besides the database component. For example, if multiple programming languages are used, this can create parsing difficulty when generating RTF files for the linguists. The most common programming languages that are found on most websites are JavaScript, Perl, ASP, ColdFusion, and PHP.

Last, but far from least, working on the graphical assets of a website can be difficult when source materials (Photoshop, Illustrator, or CorelDraw files) are not available. Nothing is worse than being asked to recreate localized versions of these elements with their omnipresent gradient backgrounds and obscure fonts. This invariably requires design expertise from (and budget for) our DTP department.

Repeat after us: It is always a good idea to keep the source files in a safe place, and to isolate localizable layers. This useful feature is offered by both Photoshop and Illustrator.

Talking the Talk: Terminology Management and Translation Memory

The last function that a localization engineer performs may be the most important. Terminology management, including the creation and maintenance of translation memories (TM), has a huge effect on both quality and consistency. It may also be the single most important factor in reducing localization costs.

Translation memories are a must-have for any localization project. Some localization firms assign the task of terminology control to the project manager. We believe in using the right person for the job and when it comes to managing hundreds of multilingual translation memories, we have no doubt that this person is the localization engineer. An inaccurate or corrupted TM (whether it is a linguistic corruption or an encoding corruption) can reduce leveraging, adding to the project's cost and ultimately hurting the quality of the translation.

There are several big players in the TM tool market. The largest market share currently belongs to TRADOS. Its emerging competitor is SDLX. A few other smaller, more specialized players like DéjàVu and TermStar are also worth mentioning. The principle behind each of these products is the same: the translator uses the tool interactively within a word processor to automatically retrieve existing translations from a database (translation memory). For localization engineers, it does not really matter which tool is used since most, if not all, of them are TMX compliant, meaning that the TM content can be exchanged between CAT tools through an XML-based export file (TMX file). All of them also offer fuzzy matching, which gives the translator close matches to a localizable sentence, thereby speeding up the translation.

Although TMs are not the most challenging aspect of the localization engineer's job, they are definitely the backbone of any localization process.

Another linguistic tool that is often integral to the development and maintenance of an effective TM is glossary management. In the world of localization, glossaries represent a list of key terms and definitions that the translator will need to properly localize the source materials. Many of the TM tools include a glossary management module to facilitate the compilation of a glossary and the subsequent translation of the key terms whenever (and wherever) they appear. These modules, such as MultiTerm from TRADOS, run in the background as the translation is being done in a word processing application. They then flag for the linguist any term that is located in the MultiTerm glossary, minimizing the time a linguist typically needs to go back and forth between reference materials and applications.

The newest glossary management tools are so customizable that they even allow the user to add multimedia content to the term definition. The possibilities are infinite. The next generation of translation tools will even allow localization vendors to share their glossaries, as well as their translation memories, over the Internet (both TRADOS and SDL have such solutions), which greatly facilitates the interaction between the localization company, the client, the linguists, and the in-country reviewer.

Chapter 7: Engineering

Wrapping Up

Look, let's speak plainly. Localization engineering is not rocket science—but in our estimation, it comes close. As you prepare for a localization project, be sure to leave a seat at the table for an engineer. From the initial internationalization planning, through the actual translation and implementation stages, and finally the on-going translation memory development and maintenance, an engineer will be directly involved. We may be biased, but we believe that a top-notch engineering department can anticipate the potential issues you may face well ahead of time: from nagging technical oddities to esoteric cultural differences. So, as you plan your next project, keep us engineers in mind. The extra time you invest up front will pay off in terms of reduced timelines and cost savings in the long run.

From David Ordoubadian: "Here's my favorite from personal experience. At 4:30 on a Friday afternoon I received a phone call from a printer I'd worked with in the past. He had received an ad leaflet from a client that was in English and for immediate printing, but he suspected there were problems with the language so he asked me if he could fax it over for review. I agreed to stay in later to get the job to him. When it arrived, I saw it was from a company that produces nozzles for vacuum cleaners. It read: 'Try the Twinner, a new Swedish innovation who really sucks.'"

Chapter 8: Quality Assurance - How to be Certain You Got it Right

Cristina Tacconi
Quality Assurance Supervisor/Italian Linguist

Cristina was born in Varese, Italy, and she has lived in the USA for 15 years. She has been with Lingo Systems for over eight years, and she is in charge of the Quality Assurance Department. "We take a lot of pride in what we do here," she says. "We make sure that our translated projects resemble exactly (in every aspect but the language) the original source provided by our clients. My team and I share the same philosophy: Quality is our number one priority, and the main reason why our clients love us and keep coming back to us."

As you already know from writing and producing your English documentation, websites or software, the quality of the writing and the presentation are extremely important in achieving product acceptance. How many times have you laughed over incomprehensible instructions for connecting a new audio system or assembling a new toy for your child? You would hate to have someone laugh over something you or your company produced. The same quality requirements are applicable to localization. If you are going to the trouble of translating and localizing your product, you want that product to meet your quality expectations and those of your target audience. You also want that product to reflect the carefully crafted image that you convey to the marketplace.

Think Quality From the Start

To maximize quality, you should consider reviewing your source content and product(s) to determine whether they are "localization-ready" even before the translation process begins (i.e., while your materials are still in development). The purpose of this review is to identify possible issues that may affect successful localization. You probably are familiar with the concept of internationalizing software (preparing software so that it can be easily localized in the future). We would encourage you to apply that same idea to *all* of your products, including documentation. In our experience, this important step is often overlooked in documentation development, resulting in timelines that do not allow for thorough internationalization prior to commencing the project.

Chapter 8: Quality Assurance

To help you in preparing your documentation for localization, your localization provider should offer to review or "clean up" your English documentation, making it more suitable for localization. An English document that is grammatically correct and free from inconsistencies in terminology greatly facilitates the translation process. Similarly, consistent formatting style (see Chapter 10) greatly improves the document localization process. Keep in mind that a poorly formatted paragraph that requires desktop publishing correction will need to be fixed for *each* language if you wait until after the translation process is completed. If you review and clean up the document before translation begins the offending paragraph need only be repaired once!

Thinking about your quality needs and document localization issues early in the development process can only improve your final product. The more thought you put into preparing your products for subsequent localization, the more likely you are to end up with higher quality, lower costs, and shorter timelines.

Quality Assurance

Quality needs are somewhat subjective, and can vary depending upon the use of the final product. If you are creating consumer products, you may have very exacting quality standards, whereas for an in-house training course your quality requirements may be more relaxed. When we talk about Quality Assurance (QA) with regard to localized materials, we are looking at three main areas:

- Translation quality (how effectively the source content is translated into each language),
- Visual review (whether the document conforms to the look and feel of the original source materials),
- Functional testing (whether your software, website, and on-screen displays function properly in the target-market technical environment).

On a Japanese food processor: "Not to be used for the other use."

The Guide to Translation and Localization

Chapter 8: Quality Assurance

Barbara Bonnema
Quality Assurance Specialist/Dutch Linguist

I can go Dutch and not have to pay a cent. I don't bake Dutch apple pie, even in a Dutch oven. I don't need a Heineken to have Dutch courage. My mom and my dad are both from Holland, so I guess that makes me Double Dutch. Born and raised in the Netherlands, now I live in another land, wielding my merciless red pen for the forces of Gouda. Who am I? I'm the little Dutch girl who came to stay.

Translation Quality

Many factors impact linguistic quality. They include:

- Who performs the translations (professionals vs. non-professionals),
- Number of linguistic steps (one, two, or three),
- In-country review,
- Use of linguistic tools (style guidelines, glossary, terminology list), and
- Use of software tools (e.g., TRADOS).

A comprehensive discussion of each of these items is presented in Chapters 6 and 7. To a large extent, however, they are all an important part of the quality assurance process. For example, performing additional linguistic steps to copy edit the work of a translator, or proofreading the draft output for consistency and flow of language will improve quality and ensure accuracy. Similarly, utilizing your own in-country personnel or representatives to review the final deliverable is another QA procedure that will further enhance overall quality.

Functional Testing

Online Documentation

As with your printed documentation, any online documentation should also be validated in a QA review. The two main online documentation formats in use today, Portable Document Format (PDF) files and HTML files, also require functional testing to confirm that they work the way they are intended to on the software platforms used in your target markets. These tests, which are typically performed by your localization vendor or a testing and integration company, should be performed on computers running native operating systems to ensure that the functionality and character displays are correct. Typically, the files are checked for:

- Compatibility with native operating systems,
- Correct display of fonts and graphics within appropriate browser or reader,
- Correct function of hyperlinks, and
- Clear printing of pages.

This list may be customized with other items, depending upon any advanced features that may be added to the PDF or HTML files.

Software and User Interfaces (GUI)

Software and other User Interfaces (GUI) also require a thorough QA review. This testing process is similar to PDF and HTML testing. Software should be checked on native operating systems to ensure that character encoding and fonts are correct, and that any text expansion does not result in truncated text strings. In addition, hotkeys and keyboard shortcuts need to be tested to make sure there are no conflicts and that the keys used actually appear on the local keyboard. Finally, the application needs to be tested to ensure that the localization process did not introduce any bugs into the software. Typically, software should go through a full regression test to make sure that all areas of the software perform as intended. As with HTML and PDF testing, the actual test may be altered to suit a specific need or client request.

A more complete discussion on testing and integration can be found in Chapter 16.

Visual Review

Once the formal translation process has come to an end, the quality assurance process continues in different forms, depending on the nature of your project.

If your project includes printed materials, the QA reviewers perform visual validation to ensure that everything in the translated document matches the source document (usually the original English text). The QA reviewer validates items such as:

- Completed translation (all items that should be translated are translated, and those that should remain in the source language are not translated),
- Consistent font type, style, and size,
- Correct placement and size of graphics,
- Graphic content (making sure there is no "clipping" of graphic or text elements),
- Page flow and page numbering,
- Cross-references between text and the table of contents, indices, internal references, screen captures, and/or graphic caption text, and
- Text indentation and alignment.

Chapter 8: Quality Assurance

This list can expand considerably, and is normally customized for each project, based on input from the client. To help your vendor develop quality guidelines, it is a good idea to provide them with any information that can aid the translation and QA steps early in the localization process. Some examples of helpful information to provide to your vendor include:

- Terms and names that are to remain in English,
- A list of part numbers for your products,
- Measurement units and conversions to be used in your document (inches/mm, pounds/grams, Celsius/Fahrenheit, etc.), and
- Local contact information for each language (phone numbers, addresses, email addresses, website URLs, etc.).

Summary

When selecting a localization vendor, you will want to hire a firm that cares as much as you do about carefully reproducing, in different languages, what took you so much time and effort to create in the first place. A good way to determine this is to inquire about a potential vendor's QA procedures. There are many translators and many translation companies on the market, but not all of them maintain the same quality standards for their work. Quality assurance steps must be implemented at each stage of a project in order for a localization vendor to deliver the final product exactly as you requested.

In an Acapulco restaurant: "The manager has personally passed all the water served here."

Chapter 9: Formatting Print and Online Documents

Desktop publishing is an important part of many localization projects. It is not enough to simply translate the words and let them fall where they may. Care must be taken to present your localized manuals and help systems with the same sense of style and polish that they have in their source language. Fortunately, the latest technology makes this task much easier. In this chapter, we will review both printed and online documentation, the changing nature of fonts, the wiles of text expansion, resizing screen captures, and portable documents. We end with a look at the tools that have revolutionized technical writing: single-source and content management.

Experience Counts

Localization vendors handle desktop publishing in one of three ways: some use their own employees, others outsource to contractors (either off-shore or on-shore), and the rest subcontract with the translation agencies who perform the linguistic work.

The differences can be significant, so do your homework. A skilled formatter knows many ways to ensure that your materials look as good in the new language as they did in the original. Also, with expertise comes efficiency. While the neophyte is searching for some way to squeeze text elegantly, the old pro simply reaches into a bag of trusted tricks. You shouldn't have to pay for someone else's on-the-job training.

Roger Thompson
DTP Supervisor

Roger belongs to the family Myrmeleontidae. The name is rooted in the Greek words myrmex (ant) and leon (lion). The family Myrmeleontidae is part of the order Neuroptera, translated variously as "nerve wings," "net wings," or "sinew wings." All Neuroptera have four wings marked by a netlike pattern of veins. The order Neuroptera, which includes dobsonflies and lacewings, is the most primitive order of insects with complete metamorphosis. A lot of people don't know that.

The best way to ensure that you receive well-formatted deliverables is to ask for references and check them out. Inquire as to how many years of experience the formatters have with the desktop publishing program you use. If the job requires a new program or a new version of a traditional program, make sure the vendor knows how to use it, and that they have the appropriate target language version. Since the formatting for some languages can only be done on a native operating system, your vendor will need to have invested in a variety of systems and licensed publishing tools. Even experienced formatters can get lost when working with other languages if they are only familiar with their native tongue. On the other hand, experienced localization vendors will already have dealt with most system, application, and file compatibility issues. If you are invited to visit the vendor's site, ask for a tour and a demonstration of capabilities.

Selecting the Right Font

Software fonts have been around for more than twenty years. The earliest versions were sufficient to display text in dot patterns on monitors and dot matrix printers. Most did not have an extended character set to display accented characters, which is a fundamental requirement for localized documents. Even today, some of the new specialty fonts do not feature even the simplest accented vowels. If you use one of these fonts, it will probably have to be replaced in order to display other languages.

Multilingual fonts were first included with the Windows operating system in the mid-nineties. If the target languages were European, Slavic, Baltic, Cyrillic, or Turkic, the available fonts in the Windows character map application would probably suffice. Double-byte languages were another matter. Hebrew, Arabic, Hindi, and most Asian languages required font substitution even when Windows multilingual fonts were used.

The twenty-first century has seen a breakthrough in software fonts with the inclusion of Unicode in the Windows XP and Macintosh OS X operating systems. Because Unicode fonts use more bytes per character, most alphabets around the world can be represented. Even if an operating system supports Unicode fonts, however, there are still some desktop publishing applications that do not accommodate them. Eventually, all software fonts will be Unicode and applications that do not display them will be defunct.

Fonts can also be an issue when making PDF (Portable Document Format) files. In the early nineties, some font manufacturers took pains to prevent their fonts from being embedded out of the fear that hackers would be able to extract them from the PDFs. This concern never materialized because the effort did not equal the prize. But, if a document uses one of these older fonts and you wish to make it portable, consider changing to a different font.

Text Expansion

When English is translated into other languages, it often takes more space to say the same thing. The reason may be that the new language uses more articles, as in French or Italian, or because the words are simply longer, as in Dutch or German. On the other hand, the new language might use a few ideograms to express an entire phrase causing the opposite effect. While text contraction is rarely a problem when localizing documents, text expansion can raise some tricky issues. The standard rule of thumb in the localization industry is that European languages can expand, on average, by about thirty percent (without hyphenation). This can cause several challenges. A table that fits on one page in English may spill over to the top of the next page in Greek. Similarly, section headings in large type might run to two lines. Indented text could leave large blocks of white space to the left.

At the beginning of the localization project, your provider should ask questions to determine how you want to handle text expansion. Do you want to shrink the font to ensure that pagination, table of contents entries, and index references match the English source document? If so, should the line spacing (or kerning) shrink proportionally? Or would you prefer to keep the same font sizes and allow the text to flow, increasing the page count? Can formatters borrow space from the margins? Can the indentations be shrunk to reduce white space to the left? Can headings be made smaller? If so, should changes affect all similar headings or only those that present a problem? When long words expand to accomplish full justification, the spacing between the letters can stretch in ways that are uncomfortable to read. Can justification be turned off? What about hyphenation? Should hyphenation be turned on or off? By addressing these layout concerns at the beginning of the project, your localized documents will have much higher quality when they are delivered.

The table to the right presents an interesting look at one study on text expansion. While the information is informative, the percentage can change significantly depending on how you decide to handle compound words and hyphenation.

TEXT EXPANSION/ CONTRACTION	
Language	% difference
Arabic	104 %
Chinese	61 %
Czech	117 %
Dutch	128 %
English	100%
Esperanto	92 %
Farsi	104 %
Finnish	103 %
French	111 %
German	108 %
Greek	128 %
Hebrew	83 %
Hindi	83 %
Hungarian	113 %
Italian	109 %
Japanese	115 %
Korean	123 %
Portuguese	110 %
Russian	115 %
Spanish	117 %
Swahili	88 %
Swedish	95 %

(George Sadek & Maxim Zhukov, Typographia polyglotta, New York: ATypI /Cooper Union, 1997. The study compared the Preamble from the Universal Declaration of Human Rights in a variety of languages, with English as the base 100 %.)

If your text does expand when translated, you will need to decide whether the localized documents should maintain the same page breaks and the same total number of pages as the English source document. It is generally easier, and therefore less expensive, if page breaks can flow during the localization process. From the perspective of customer support, however, it is often preferable for the localized manuals to match the page breaks in the English version so that support personnel can easily refer to "page 37 of the manual" for solving a problem. If page break matching between languages is necessary, it is very important to allow for extra white space in the original version. Matching page breaks from source to target documents can add to the cost of the project, especially when the source document does not allow sufficient white space for text expansion.

Online Documentation

Online documentation avoids some of the pitfalls of text expansion and page matching that are associated with printed materials, but it introduces engineering issues. For example, if your document is displayed on a computer screen in HTML, WinHelp or some other online format, expansion will not be a problem since the text will extend downward and the user simply scrolls down the page to read the expanded text. What can be an issue is whether or not the content displays correctly on the operating systems and typical viewing applications (browsers) available in your target market. By performing functional testing on native operating systems, your localization provider will be able to ensure that the applications perform and display as advertised. Be sure to discuss your specific engineering testing requirements with your localization vendor so that you are both clear on testing expectations.

Resizing Graphics and Forms

Online forms and other page elements that contain text such as graphics and buttons may also need to be resized after translation. Similarly, online forms may require special engineering to support the user's ability to enter special characters, international style phone numbers, and foreign addresses (along with any other special requirements of your international users).

Chapter 9: Formatting & Publishing

Screen Captures

Almost all software documentation uses screen captures, which are graphics or pictures of the software as displayed on screen. This has become a technical documentation convention for tying together the references in the document to the items the user sees on screen.

Just as translated text expands in the body of the document, translated dialog boxes in GUI applications must expand as well. One of the most common examples is an error message box. A screen capture of an error message that was originally 432 pixels wide (6 inches on a 72 dpi Mac system), might need to be expanded to 504 pixels (7 inches) to fit the translated text. In the documentation, the 7-inch screen capture must be resized to fit in the same space as the original 6-inch screen capture. This often leads to distorted or fuzzy images. To solve this problem, the screen capture can be left at 7 inches (possibly throwing off the formatting), resized to something that causes less distortion, or used at 6 inches, accepting the distortions. If your document uses screen captures, be prepared to talk with your localization vendor about how you would like these matters resolved.

It is also important that the screen captures of your localized software be taken on a localized operating system. If a question is asked in French, the *yes* and *no* buttons should be French as well.

Portable Document Format (PDF)

With the advent of PDFs, documents became fully "portable" with their original layout and design remaining intact. Over time, PDFs have become specialized according to how they will be viewed. A high resolution PDF is necessary for high-quality offset printing, while a low resolution electronic book is best for distribution over the Internet. A print-quality PDF is usually huge in file size, often over 100 MB while an online PDF can be as small as 1 MB or less. In both cases, the fonts must be embedded. Another version is a functional PDF, which contains bookmarks, links, and can even launch other applications. It is important to indicate which kind of PDF you want at the beginning of your project.

The Guide to Translation and Localization

Chapter 9: Formatting & Publishing

Single-Source Content Management

Pete Landers
DTP Specialist

Pete first fell in love with other languages when he heard opera in grade school. Phrases like "Vesti la giubba," "Mi chiamo Mimi," or "Celeste Aida" still conjure images of far-off adventure for him. After several years in book distribution, arts administration, and technical writing, Pete came to Lingo Systems to use his layout skills on multilingual subjects. Even though the text may be referring to a wrench or process management, somehow the fact that it is in another language makes him think it is romantic. If you catch him singing "Per stringere, girare la vite in senso orario," don't tell him it only means "To tighten, turn the screw clockwise."

The concept of single-sourcing predates true content management. As the words suggest, it means writing one document and using that to produce more than one output. With the use of hidden text, variables, conditional text, and export filters, a desktop publisher is able to publish to multiple media, including hardcopy documents, web pages, electronic books, help files, and more.

Single-sourcing can be as simple as using the "Save As..." command from MS Word to create web pages. In this case the source is the Word file and the hardcopy and web page are two different outputs from the same (single) source. Anyone with a copy of MS Word on their computer can accomplish this. If the web pages are subsequently imported into a help system, you now have a third use of the same material. When localized, only the Word file is translated. The original file then becomes a translation memory (TM) from which many other deliverables can be produced.

If your publishing requirements involve anything beyond limited Word documents, or if localization is in your future, the quick-fix described above will not be sufficient. Thankfully, far more powerful and sophisticated single-source and content management solutions are currently available. These range from off-the-shelf single-source publishing programs to highly customizable, enterprise-level content management systems.

For single-source publishing, Quadralay Corporation's suite of WebWorks products enables users to convert output from MS Word or FrameMaker into HTML, WinHelp, HTML Help, or even XML. The real tricks are in what can be done with the text as it passes through WebWorks. For example, a skilled user can map the styles in your source to any other style in a cascading style sheet. Or, you can create character maps to match special, and extended characters to their corresponding HTML codes. As with any application, the more features it has, the more complicated it is to use. Fortunately, WebWorks comes with some templates that can be used for simple operations. Macromedia's RoboHelp product has similar output capabilities, and has traditionally been popular with help authors.

Chapter 9: Formatting & Publishing

A single-source solution that also includes content management may be appropriate if, in addition to multiple outputs, your publishing environment includes any of the following:

- Multiple content authors,
- A desire to publish in many languages,
- A high degree of similarity between content, and
- Difficulty in managing version control.

Not too long ago, content management systems were practically unobtainable for all but the largest corporations. Now, state of the art applications such as AuthorIT, Documentum, and Interwoven (to name a few) use either object-oriented, or relational database architecture, to combine multi-media publishing capability with authoring, version control, file sharing, and a host of other features. Perhaps the best news is that there are content management systems to fit virtually any budget, from highly customizable enterprise applications to entry level systems, with lots of functionality.

The need to provide clients with localized content is a major factor for companies moving toward content management systems. These tools provide a framework for creating and maintaining control of multi-language content—and thus minimizing cost. A more thorough discussion of single-source content management tools is presented in Chapter 14 by Paul Trotter, CEO of AuthorIT Software Corporation.

From Anna Kuzminsky: "Here is one of my favorites: On a multilingual airline menu the dessert was 'sponge cake' and the translation into Swedish stated it as 'svampkaka'. Sponge in Swedish means something that you use to clean with (kitchen or yourself), but that word is also the same as the translation for 'mushroom'. Another favorite is the translation of 24/7 to July 24th."

The Guide to Translation and Localization

Chapter 10: Writing for Localization - Advice for Technical Writers

Willy van Grunsven
Co-Owner/Client Services Manager

Willy came to America on the SS Amsterdam. After setting off from her native Holland, the ship became horribly lost in a dense layer of sea foam while rounding the southern tip of Northern Ireland. The ship docked on an unfamiliar coastline many weeks later. When the locals were asked where they had landed, the answer was given in a strange and exotic language. After a long while of gesturing and grunting it was finally determined that they had landed in "America, land of the Free, home of the Brave." Determined that no one should ever have to communicate in such a way again, Willy set about teaching and helping others to communicate globally. The rest, as they say, is history.

Technical writers play a crucial role in the product development process. They are responsible for writing the content that describes your products to your end user. Technical writers develop printed documentation, online documentation (such as help files and functional PDF files), and website content. They must take the technical knowledge imparted to them by product developers and present it clearly and concisely to your less technically savvy consumers. This is, as you can well imagine, not an easy task.

When taking your products to the global marketplace, an additional burden is placed on your technical writers. While they are preparing documentation for your US release they must also *keep in mind the requirements for simultaneous or subsequent localization*. As defined in Chapter 2, the process of developing a product for both US and overseas markets at the same time is called internationalization.

Documentation that has been properly internationalized is easier, less costly, and more efficient to localize. Not only will this reduce your localization costs, but it could result in huge indirect savings as well. Shorter timelines often mean a faster release to market and accelerated revenue streams.

Some of the tips that can help your company realize these benefits are described in the following sections.

Layout Issues: Allow for Text Expansion

It is vitally important that your document's layout leave enough room (i.e., white space) for the inevitable text expansion that occurs during the localization process. This cannot be overemphasized. Formatting the translated document is far easier, and more efficient when adequate space is available. Formatting costs can rise dramatically when the translated text must be laboriously manipulated to fit within a cramped space. A comprehensive discussion on text expansion is included in Chapter 9.

Graphic Considerations: Separate Text from Graphics

Ideally, graphics should not contain text for the simple reason that it eliminates the need to translate them. If text must be associated with a graphic, try to create the text as a separate component in the page-layout application (e.g., FrameMaker, QuarkXpress, InDesign) used to create the document. That is, a callout or caption for a graphic should ideally be a text block in the layout program, not an element of an Illustrator Encapsulated Postscript (EPS) file. This requires less work to localize (saving you money), as the graphic text is part of the main document text, and not a layer inside the graphic file.

If you must include text in EPS graphic files, remember to leave it in text form. Do not outline the text, as this makes it very difficult and time-consuming to retype, and translate.

Screen captures are a special category of graphics. By their very nature they contain text. Translation of screen capture text is accomplished through localization of the software that was used to generate the English captures. Once the software is localized, the screen captures are regenerated. When developing application software, be aware of how the text fits in various windows. Avoid packing text too tightly; it will expand when the software is localized. When creating the screen captures in English, be sure to generate all of them at the same screen resolution and scale, and then save the files in the same format used by the document layout application. You will also want to employ a logical naming convention that will help identify where screen captures are placed.

Aerolinea Danese: "We take your bags and send them in all directions."

Chapter 10: Writing Tips

Dianne Ellis
DTP Specialist

Chocolate, cioccolate, chocolat, yuch, Schokolade, chocolade, czekolada: I believe chocolate in any language or format can solve any problem on earth. Chocolate is made up of about 300 chemicals, such as caffeine, theobromine, and phenyethylamine, and is thought to have mood-altering effects. I just know that if I put "eat chocolate" at the top of my to-do list every day, I'll get at least one thing done.

Limit Your Font Types and Font Faces

When selecting fonts for a new document destined for translation, remember that simpler is better. Some languages contain a multitude of accents and special characters that can become illegible if overly ornate or decorative fonts are used. The conventional combination of a standard serif font (e.g., Times) for body copy and a standard sans serif font (e.g., Helvetica) for headings is a good example of font selections that work well for translation. In general, stick to fonts that are clean and crisply drawn, avoiding fonts with exceptionally thin serifs or wispy details.

You should also try to keep the total number of fonts used in the document to a manageable number—no more than three or four. Ideally, select fonts that are available on both PC and Macintosh platforms. This facilitates the easy movement of the document across platforms, if required, during localization.

As a general rule, custom or proprietary fonts can be problematic. They are often expensive and/or difficult to acquire. If required in the final deliverable for branding purposes, expect to provide them to your localization provider. Not only will it reduce time and expense, but you will be sure to get the exact font you need.

Some languages require extended character sets that provide accented letters such as "ç." Bear in mind that many specialized fonts do not support languages other than English because they lack this extended character set, so select your fonts carefully. Still other languages need special fonts that are not available as extended character sets. For example, Japanese, Korean, Traditional and Simplified Chinese are considered "double-byte languages," which means that each written character contains two bytes (16 bits) of data instead of 1 byte (8 bits). This used to cause problems for applications and operating systems that did not support double-byte characters. Fortunately, today's operating systems and the applications that run on them use Unicode. Unicode supports the double-byte character sets, as well as all other character sets directly, making the display of foreign characters much easier.

Character styles used in Western European or US English layouts are not always transferable to Asian languages. In many cases they are not used at all. For instance, character styles such as bold and italic are not always applicable to Asian type styles. Furthermore, Asian characters do not distinguish between upper and lowercase. For design purposes, the best way to distinguish Asian characters from surrounding text is to vary the font face or weight (e.g., using a heavier version of a typeface for added emphasis). Your localization provider should offer a variety of techniques to help keep the look and feel in your Asian product as you originally intended.

Internationalize Your Templates

If you use templates and associated scripts to provide a standard look and feel for your layout, it is important to consider localization issues when designing that template. Scripts that automatically capitalize titles, for example, rarely work correctly on translated content (as the capitalization rules vary by language). So keep your target languages in mind. Isolate text and automate formatting in clearly identified sections of the template so that your localization provider can easily find them.

Develop a Glossary

Glossaries help linguists understand any industry- or product-specific terms you may use in your writing. As you write, keep a separate list of terms that have special meanings. Providing these terms, and their definitions to your localization provider at the beginning of the project results in a much higher quality product at the end. See Chapter 6 for more detailed information about glossaries.

Write Marketing Materials with Localization in Mind

Marketing materials may require special handling. They do not always localize easily. The text and images that succinctly communicate your company or product to an American audience may not be relevant in Europe or Asia. We are all familiar with the stories about product names that take on a second meaning when introduced in another market. If possible, create your marketing material with localization in mind, and keep the content as precise and globally understandable as possible. If this is not possible, be prepared to provide explanatory material that will help provide the background, concept, and context behind your marketing campaign. At this point, localization may become less about straightforward translation, and more about creating the same idea or impression while using a different concept all together. This is where your localization partner will prove their expertise, and become invaluable to you.

Remember Your International Audience

When developing your content, avoid using slang terms and culturally biased graphics. Slang is difficult to translate and understand in a foreign context. Similarly, graphics can also have a cultural bias that is difficult to understand. A bunny rabbit might be used in an English document to represent *fast* but to the French it looks like dinner!

Write Out Acronyms

Write out the meaning of all acronyms when they first appear in the source documentation. Later, when translated, the first use of the acronym should be both defined and translated in the target language, even if the acronym remains in its English form throughout the document.

Monitor Your Word Count

The cost of localization is directly related to the number of words you write: more words mean higher costs. Monitor your documentation word count by using the "Word Count" command found in your development software. Keep sentence structure and grammar simple and vocabulary choices clear.

Use Repetitions in Your Documentation

The cost for localization can also be lowered by including repetitions in your documentation. Most localization providers use tools to help identify text that can be leveraged, that is, once translated it can be re-used either within the same document or in subsequent versions (see Chapter 7 for more details about translation tools). Although you may earn style points for finding new and different ways to say the same thing every time a phrase or concept appears in your English source document, you might also surpass your budget by doing so. Including lots of repetitions in the text will increase the leveraging percentages, which, in turn, can substantially lower localization costs.

Various Output and Content Re-use

Many companies make their documentation available to customers in both a paper-based medium, and an electronic form, such as HTML and PDF formats. Other companies have opted to save the printing and distribution charges associated with hardcopy manuals, and rely solely on the electronic versions. Both HTML and PDF formats are widely used on the Internet and alternative media such as distribution CDs, because they appear virtually the same regardless of the operating system the customer uses to view them. For complex, inter-related documents, HTML and PDF formats also offer the advantage of incorporating hypertext—clicking on a cross-reference, index, or table of contents entry that takes the user immediately to the relevant entry.

Chapter 10: Writing Tips

The advent of single-source and content management technologies has everyone thinking about content re-use. For FrameMaker users, it is now possible to structure a document that contains all of your print and online help content, and use single-source publishing tools to publish this content as print documentation, online (HTML-based) documentation, help files, and functional PDF's.
Each published output may use all of the original content, or just a subset that can be selected using conditional text. Similarly, XML-based content management systems allow you to store content "chunks" in a database structure, and to publish your deliverables from those chunks. Both processes are great for localization because translation only has to occur once for use in many outputs. See Chapter 14 for more information about single-source content management. Although these tools may offer substantial savings in time, effort, and money, they also require careful planning before starting the process. Creating modular content repositories (be they for single-source applications or complete content management systems) takes planning to create a logical structure that is easy to reference.

When generating electronic documents, you want the output style to convey the same structured sense of importance that was incorporated in the print document. Moreover, a document that does not use style tags efficiently (i.e., one that uses a different style tag each time to produce exactly the same formatting attributes), requires much more time to set up than a document that uses only one style tag to represent this uniform style. Using consistent style definitions throughout your document allows both PDF bookmark data and HTML style tags to be generated in the localized files more easily.

Mercedes –Benz shortened the name of their Grand Sport Tourer, which debuts in 2005, to the succinct GST. The French don't have a problem with those initials, but in Canada GST is the acronym for the widely loathed goods and services tax.

Chapter 11: Same Language, Different Dialect

Winston Churchill once described the US and the UK as two countries separated by a common language. In translation, a similar challenge arises when writing for other languages:

- Spanish readers in Madrid vs. Mexico City, or Los Angeles,
- French readers in Paris vs. Montreal,
- Portuguese readers in Lisbon vs. Rio, and
- Chinese readers in Beijing vs. Hong Kong.

Spanish (Iberian vs. Latin)

Spanish localization represents one of the most obvious opportunities to expand the market for your products. More than 330 million people around the world use Spanish as their native language. In the US alone, roughly 40 million residents primarily speak Spanish, and that number is expected to grow substantially in the coming years.

The fact that Spanish is spoken so widely poses an interesting challenge for localization because the language has evolved in each region of the world. Spanish translators typically make a distinction between Iberian (Spain) and Latin (the Americas) Spanish. The differences are further compounded, however, when examined on a country-by-country basis. Although the broad brush of Latin Spanish includes Argentina, Columbia, Mexico, Cuba, and Puerto Rico (to name a few), there are clear linguistic variations and peculiarities that characterize each—with the greatest being pronunciation.

The glue that keeps the Spanish language together as one linguistic unit is the Real Academia de la Lengua Española (Royal Academy of the Spanish Language). The Royal Academy sets the standards of the Spanish language for all the Spanish-speaking countries in the world. Their decisions are meticulously observed by those who teach, write, or are in any way involved with the use and implementation of the Spanish language.

Chapter 11: Different Dialects

Eric Manning
Senior Project Manager

Eric Manning's gripping third novel combines a Joycean ear for language with Henry James's eye for detail and Lewis Carroll's flair for quirky problem-solving. Manning conjures a world in which John Lennon is a patron saint, pigs can talk, and television is regulated as a controlled substance. The plot is too complex to recount here but is essentially beside the point anyway; just let yourself get caught up in the dizzying array of offbeat characters and oddball situations portrayed by this transplanted East Coaster. It's my *must-read* pick for the summer.

Given the lasting impact of their decisions, the Royal Academy is painstakingly slow in reaching those decisions. While the arbiters of new terminology may proceed at a very slow and cautious rate, technology races along. Until the Royal Academy decides each issue, the Spanish translator is forced to make his or her own decisions on terminology. Experienced translators are always careful to use terms that are understood by the greatest number of users, regardless of their location.

If Spanish has a regulating body that decides all matters concerning written Spanish (grammar, syntax, spelling, etc.), then why do some people believe that there are different kinds of Spanish? As noted above, the greatest differences exist in the way words are spoken and the way certain letters are pronounced (or maybe not pronounced). Thus, in certain parts of Spain, the letter "z" is pronounced as a soft English "th" as in the word "thin," whereas, in Latin America the letter "z" is always pronounced as an "s" as in "Sam." However, whether in Argentina, Mexico, or Madrid, the word "zapato" (shoe) must always be written with a "z." Local differences can also be found in the use of certain nouns—especially those that designate agricultural products: the English say "potato," Latin America prefers "papa," and Spain "patata."

Geography can also play a role in the determination of terminology. With their geographical proximity to the United States, some Latin American countries identify more closely with terms used in the United States and "Spanish-ize" the terms. A good example is the word "computer." In most Latin American countries "computer" is rendered as "computadora." In Spain, because of its proximity to France, "computer" is rendered as "ordenador," from the French "ordinateur." However, geographical proximity is not always the determining factor; take, for example, the English term "font." Latin America prefers "tipo" or "fuente," while Spain has kept the English word "font."

While these examples contrast Iberian and Latin American Spanish, other linguistic differences occur within Latin America. Chile, Columbia, and Argentina usually identify more closely with Europe than the United States, yet the rule is not hard and fast. The decimal and thousand separators are good examples. Mexico, Central America, and some South American countries use these separators in the same way as the United States (where one thousand twenty is represented 1,020.00). Chile, Columbia, and Argentina prefer the European way of expressing separators (where one thousand twenty is represented 1.020,00).

In the United States, the situation is even more complicated as Spanish speakers have emigrated from many different countries and brought their regionalisms with them. How, then, can you choose the best *regional* form of Spanish?

Chapter 11: Different Dialects

Fortunately, there is a relatively simple solution to this problem: Use Spanish translators with extensive experience. Experienced translators avoid the colloquialisms and regionalisms that are used in some countries, but not in others; instead, they use terms that are understood by the vast majority of readers. As a result, you will find that after translation and editing, there will be no difference between Mexican, Puerto Rican, Costa Rican, Argentinian, and Iberian Spanish.

Portuguese (Portugal vs. Brazil)

Nearly 210 million people speak Portuguese throughout the world today. However, spoken Portuguese is not homogeneous. It differs in grammar, pronunciation, and vocabulary among Portuguese speakers in Portugal and in Brazil.

Brazilian Portuguese was not only influenced by native languages such as Tupinambá, but also by the many languages spoken by African slaves. Although some Brazilian words made their way to Europe, most were only used in Brazil. Southern Brazil absorbed a large influx of immigrants of Italian, German, and Japanese descent. These linguistic groups made several contributions to the language spoken in Brazil. Portuguese in Europe, meanwhile, was influenced by the French spoken during Napoleon's occupation of Portugal.

In the twentieth century, the linguistic split between Portuguese and Brazilian increased as the result of technological innovations that required new vocabulary. Unlike the Royal Academy of the Spanish Language, there is no similar "watch dog" to condone adopting new terminology and grammar in Portuguese.

Internet World Magazine published a list in the Brazilian edition that pointed out some of the differences:

English	European Portuguese	Brazilian Portuguese
to access	*aceder*	*acessar*
mouse	*rato*	*mouse*
screen	*ecrã*	*tela*

The Guide to Translation and Localization

Chapter 11: Different Dialects

Yuka Hirota
Quality Assurance Specialist/Japanese Linguist

Helping companies reach new markets through localization does more than just increase their profits—it helps them become a full partner in the world economy. It enriches people's lives who might not normally have access to the particular product or service they are offering. That's one reason I enjoy the work I do at Lingo Systems. I like being a part of the global community.

Besides words that are completely different and/or are used in a completely different context between these two variants of Portuguese, there are approximately 400 words with a different spelling, and 1,500 with a different accent mark. There are also some grammatical differences.

When localizing into Portuguese, be aware of these differences. Your localization provider should distinguish between European and Brazilian Portuguese, and should use native-quality speakers from the appropriate country to localize your product. Although Portuguese speakers from both sides of the Atlantic are able to understand each other, not localizing properly can lead to confusion among your end users.

French (France vs. Canada)

There are now nearly seven million French speakers in Canada, mostly located in the province of Quebec. Over the past four hundred years, the French spoken in this region has evolved dramatically, due in large part to distance from French speakers in Europe. It is also due to close proximity to English speakers in Canada and the United States.

Canada has certainly become a prime target market for localized products. In 1988, the Canadian government passed the Official Languages Act, which conferred equal official language status to English and French. This was done in order to preserve the nation's French linguistic heritage, and to "support the development of English and French linguistic minority communities, and generally advance the equality of status and use of the English and French languages within Canadian society." As a result, all official federal government communications must be made in both languages, and government services must be available in both languages. Many commercial products follow the government's lead and provide packaging, labeling, etc., in both English and French.

Chapter 11: Different Dialects

However, if you provide European French to a Canadian audience, you may be missing the mark. Canadian and European French differ in many ways, including vocabulary. Some differences include the following:

English	**Canadian French**	**European French**
telephone handset	*le récepteur*	*le combiné*
You're welcome	*Bienvenue*	*De rien* (and several others)
blueberry	*le bleuet*	*la myrtille*
soccer	*le soccer*	*le football*
snowbank	*le banc de neige*	*la congère*
go shopping	*magasiner*	*faire des courses*

In addition, there are differences in pronunciation, in pronouns, in verbs, and in usage.

What, then, should you know when deciding whether to translate solely into French or into both French and French Canadian? French Canadians understand any material translated in French, since the written language is generally similar. If simple understanding is your goal, the expense of translating into both French and French Canadian may not be necessary.

However, if you want French Canadians to feel that your product has been custom-made for them, you should translate it into French Canadian, as well, to ensure cultural sensitivity. This can usually be accomplished by having the work product of a French translator copy edited by a Canadian colleague. Most of the time, the linguistic changes are minimal, but you can then be confident that your product is indeed targeted for Canada. Localizing products in French Canadian and French is, of course, done at your discretion. But what is your competitor doing?

Chapter 11: Different Dialects

Chinese (Mandarin vs. Cantonese, Traditional vs. Simplified)

Rich Miller
Project Manager

Rich Miller—husband, father, brother, son, brother-in-law, uncle, nephew, cousin, friend, mentor, protégé, learner, teacher, project manager, formatter, entrepreneur, conservationist, outdoorsman, fisherman, photographer, hiker, climber, trainer, handler (as in dogs), driver, golfer, biker, builder, painter, computer enthusiast, musician, singer, pastor.

"Can you speak and write Chinese?" This apparently simple question can be answered by asking in turn, "Do you mean Mandarin, Hakka, Cantonese, Traditional Chinese, Simplified Chinese, or…?" It seems that there is quite a bit of confusion regarding what exactly "Chinese" means in regards to both the spoken language and the written language. Let's try to clear up some of this confusion.

First of all, spoken Chinese consists of dozens of different dialects, often mutually unintelligible from one another. Pu Tong Hua, known as *Mandarin* in most Western countries, and Cantonese are the two most widely spoken of these dialects. As early as the second century BC (during the Han Dynasty), language reforms were implemented in an attempt to standardize the language. Mandarin evolved as the official Chinese spoken language, because it was derived from the Beijing (i.e., Peking) dialect, which was taught by scholars and used by the government for nearly one thousand years. Taiwan and Singapore also use Mandarin as their official language. Cantonese, on the other hand, is a dialect widely spoken in the southern regions of China (the Guangzhou and Hong Kong areas).

Mandarin and Cantonese are the most widely spoken Chinese dialects, but they are by no means the only ones. For day-to-day conversation, many people still prefer to speak in the dialect of their respective regions. It is common to find that two people speaking two different dialects cannot communicate verbally; however, they can communicate in writing thanks to the standardization of the Traditional and Simplified writing systems.

The origin of the Chinese writing system is pictorial, dating back thousands of years. People drew pictures to express their thoughts—in short, to communicate. As you can imagine, this method of written communication was very cumbersome, making complex thoughts difficult to express. As a result, a number of reforms have been initiated to stylize and simplify the manner of writing Chinese. This has, in turn, resulted in a more uniform writing style.

Chapter 11: Different Dialects

Of all the language reforms initiated over the past two millennia, none has had a greater impact than the one carried out by the People's Republic of China (PRC) government after its establishment in 1949. The mid-twentieth century language reform simplified the characters used in the Traditional Chinese writing system by reducing the number of strokes needed to write a character. The end result was the Simplified Chinese writing system. The PRC and Singapore currently use the Simplified Chinese writing system. Hong Kong and Taiwan use the Traditional Chinese writing system; however, now that Hong Kong has been integrated into the PRC, we may see an increase in the use of Simplified Chinese there.

It is generally easier for a person who knows Traditional Chinese to understand Simplified Chinese characters than for a person who knows Simplified Chinese to understand Traditional Chinese characters. However, this is not a sure thing. Moreover, using one of the standard writing systems is still not always sufficient for proper localization. For example, the Traditional Chinese used in Taiwan is somewhat different from that used in Hong Kong. The character set is the same, but they are sometimes grouped differently to express various concepts. One example of this is the term "lunchbox." In Hong Kong, this term is expressed by pairing the character for "rice" with the character for "box;" in contrast, Taiwanese use a pair of characters that roughly translate as "convenience now." A Hong Kong reader unaware of Taiwanese culture would understand the characters but not grasp the lunchbox connotation. If you are planning to localize for the Hong Kong market or for the Singapore market, you should plan a special copy editing step in order to customize your translations for those specific markets.

Continuous efforts at language reform introduced the use of the Roman alphabet to "spell" the pronunciation of Chinese characters. The result was the standard Pin Yin spelling system that is widely used in China, Taiwan, and Singapore today.

In a Yugoslavian hotel: "The flattening of underwear with pleasure is the job of the chambermaid."

So, what is Chinese? You can see now that it really is a "blanket term" for several major dialects and two major writing systems.

Country	Spoken Language	Written Language
PRC	Mandarin	Simplified Chinese
PRC Guangzhou Province	Cantonese	Simplified Chinese
PRC Hong Kong	Cantonese	Traditional Chinese
Singapore	Mandarin	Simplified Chinese
Taiwan	Mandarin	Traditional Chinese

The next time you hear the question, "Do you speak and write Chinese?" the answer may depend on where you are or who is asking!

Japanese and Korean

Although Japanese and Korean are completely different from Chinese as spoken languages, their written alphabets do contain some Chinese characters. Koreans, for example, use Chinese characters to clarify the meaning of some words in combination with *Han-guel*, the Korean alphabet based on phonetic sounds. The Japanese, on the other hand, use three different alphabets:

- Hiragana,
- Katakana, and
- Kanji (the Japanese term for Chinese characters).

To add to the confusion, when Chinese characters are used in the Korean and Japanese alphabets, they do not necessarily have the same meaning and sound as in the Chinese alphabet.

Chapter 11: Different Dialects

Despite the significant differences between these three languages, they are similar in that they may require special handling during localization. Chinese, Japanese, and Korean, as well as other Asian languages, are composed of double-byte characters; for some localization projects, special software and methodology is required to handle double-byte characters. For example, while European languages can be delivered to the client with standard text flows, Asian languages may require embedded graphics to represent the text. The challenges associated with displaying and formatting Asian characters are addressed in more detail in Chapter 12. Eventually, all applications will use Unicode technology, which uses more bytes per character, and does not have these limitations.

Also, note that the syntax of Japanese and Korean phrases is ordered differently from English. Whereas, an English sentence typically begins with the subject followed by a verb and then an object, a Japanese or Korean sentence normally begins with a subject followed by an object and ends with a verb. Another difference between these two Asian languages and English is that a thought may be represented in an Asian language as a phrase or a single "word", where the English phrase is a complete sentence.

	JAPANESE	**KOREAN**	**CHINESE**
Alphabet(s) used	1) Hiragana	1) Hanguel	Chinese characters (used in different styles)
	2) Katakana	2) Han-ja (Korean term for Chinese characters)	
	3) Kanji (Japanese term for Chinese characters)		
Syntax (sentence structure)	In reverse order of English; Similar to Korean	In reverse order of English; Similar to Japanese	Similar to English

The Guide to Translation and Localization

Chapter 12: Writing and Displaying Asian Characters

Ting Fan
Systems Administrator

M OTUZQEQ ITA XAHQE OTAOAXMFQ

Hint: 01101011 01100101 01111001 00111101 00110001 00110010

Localizing into Asian languages can present unique challenges. For example, you are not likely to see a computer keyboard that contains individual keys for every Chinese or Japanese character. With more than 10,000 characters for just Chinese alone, it would have to be one really big keyboard! Fortunately, some clever methods have been devised to use the standard keyboard. Much of the discussion below, while specific to Chinese, is also applicable to Japanese and Korean.

Typing Asian Characters

In order to enter Chinese characters into a computer, you need to have an operating system that supports Chinese input methods. This could be a native Traditional or Simplified Chinese operating system, or some other OS that has either built-in support or third-party software installed for Chinese character input. Once you have the right software, there are three general methods of entering Chinese characters into a computer: typing, writing, and speaking.

The input of Chinese characters by typing involves breaking down each ideogram into a series of alphanumeric characters using a set of defined rules. These rules allow you to create the characters with a standard keyboard. This process is an input method. Numerous input methods have been developed since Chinese computing was first introduced. Two of the more popular are Cang Jie and Zhu Yin. These two methods were developed in Taiwan, and are associated with Traditional Chinese. Among older Chinese, more people use Cang Jie because that is what they learned in school. Among younger Chinese (those born after 1970), most people use Zhu Yin. The most popular input method for Simplified Chinese is Pin Yin. A person using the Cang Jie method breaks down a Chinese character into alphanumeric characters. In contrast, the Pin Yin method uses phonetics, breaking down a Chinese character by how it sounds (representing those sounds with the alphanumeric keyboard).

Chapter 12: Typing Chinese

In comparing the two methods, if you were to enter the word "Chinese" (中文), with Chang Jie, you'd type in "L" for 中 and "YK" for 文, and with Pin Yin, you'd type "zhong1 wen2" (where the number at the end of each "word" indicates the tone of that "word"). Despite the initial learning curve required to master the rules of the input systems, typing is the fastest and most effective means of inputting Chinese characters using today's technologies.

All of these input methods are supported directly by the computer operating system. Originally, because Asian characters are double-byte (see discussion below) rather than single-byte (like most "Western" alphabets) users either had to use a native operating system or purchase a third-party software bridge for an English system. Today, as a result of Unicode technology, most input methods are supported directly by Windows XP and Mac OS X even on the English version of the operating system. Moreover, with applications such as Microsoft Internet Explorer supporting double-byte web pages as well, it is (usually) pretty easy to write and display Asian double-byte characters using Western hardware and software.

Beyond these two typing methods, improvements in technology have led to new methods that do not require the mastery of the rules for input methods. For example, various companies have developed Chinese writing pads that connect directly to your computer. Users can write directly on the pad. The software recognizes the hand written characters and displays them as the appropriate type-written characters on the screen.

Another means of inputting Chinese characters derives from recent advances in speech recognition technology. Users speak directly into a microphone connected to a computer. The software then recognizes the phonetics of each word and displays the appropriate character.

These two relatively new alternative methods for the input of Chinese characters are not without drawbacks, as the interpretation of written or spoken characters is far from perfect. Also, these methods are still generally slower than the typing methods. However, as technology continues to advance, they may one day overtake the traditional typing method and allow a more convenient way of inputting Chinese characters into the computer.

Localizing Asian Software

A greater challenge sometimes arises when you localize your software. Before the advent of Unicode, some software could accept Asian input but could not display Asian characters correctly, or vice versa. Some software could do neither. To work around this limitation, a code page had to be defined in order to support certain languages. For example, Windows 95/98/Me all used code pages that contained 256 code points (one code point represents one character). For those languages with more than 256 characters, the Double-Byte Character Set (DBCS) had to be developed. A major drawback of the code page concept was that a system could only support one language at a time since the same code point may need to map to different characters for different languages. Thus, under the DBCS system, Chinese could not be mixed with Japanese within the same application. With the invention of Unicode however, these types of issues were successfully eliminated. If your application is not based on Unicode, it can still be localized, but special attention will be required. Read more about Unicode in Chapter 7 of this guide.

From Karen Sandness: "One of my recent jobs was editing a cookbook that had been translated from Japanese to English by a Japanese linguist. My favorite infelicity was his translation of the Japanese phrase for 'chicken broth' as 'broth made from chicken carcass.' I also got a chuckle out of a sign on a shop in Kyoto that sells hot, boxed lunches to go. I think the owners must have intended to write 'take out our hot stuff,' but they ended up writing, "Take out our hot staff."

Chapter 13: Localization Case Studies

Localization projects come in all shapes, sizes, and timelines. In fact, one of the most interesting parts of the localization business is the fact that no two projects are the same. While the common denominator in localization is translation of text from one language to another, everything else about individual projects varies from one to the next.

The technical requirements of the project, coupled with the client's budget and timeline, influence the way projects are executed. There is, in fact, a delicate balance among cost, timeline, and quality that controls each project. To help you better understand the dynamics among these three factors, we have summarized four types of projects below. The descriptions below represent real projects, but the identifying details have been removed to protect the innocent!

Product: Marketing Materials

Situation

Localizing marketing materials, such as print advertisements and brochures, can be one of the most difficult types of translation projects—both for linguists and clients. By definition, marketing pieces convey concepts rather than words. Thus, the best translation, even when appropriately localized so that the target audience understands what it being said, may not work from a marketing perspective. Moreover, many of the ads created in the United States use idiomatic or colloquial expressions that simply do not transfer to other languages.

Company B, a national advertising agency, regularly requests translation of the advertisements they create for their clients. In one case, they requested translation of an ad for a software company into German. The primary tag line of the ad was the idiomatic phrase, "Looks like trouble," which referred to a picture of a lion surrounded by hyenas. As is often the case with taglines, this phrase made no sense when translated directly into German.

Chapter 13: Case Studies

Ehren Schneider
Client Services Manager

Hi, I'm Charley and this is my Dad, Ehren. I think the saddest day of my life was when I realized I could beat my Dad at most things. I'll show you for a treat!

Project Scope

Documentation: 1 InDesign document containing less than 250 words.

Timeline: 1 week.

Process

When an advertising campaign is successful, multiple iterations of the same ad will be developed as the message is shaped and adjusted. Providing translations that accurately capture abstract concepts and then transferring them from one ad to the next requires a custom localization process.

In this situation, we were able to offer two very different processes to meet the unique needs of our client. Our first approach was to localize the ad to fit the target market. Thus, our linguist translated "Looks like trouble" as "Smells like fear," which kept the message consistent with the original but made it pertinent to the German market.

In addition to translating the source materials from English to the target language, we also provided a "back translation" of the localized content from the target language into English. This extra step allowed Company B to see how the original message was modified for the target market so that the changes could be reflected in subsequent iterations. Once the translation was approved, we formatted the final layout in InDesign. A draft PDF was then prepared and submitted for approval before a final High-Res PDF was created.

The other process that we proposed was to have our linguists actually write ad copy based on parameters established by the client for tone, voice, and style. Under this option, linguists would create multiple versions of an ad along with accompanying back translations. The client would then choose which message best fit their marketing strategy before moving on to final layout and delivery.

Whichever process is used, the overriding objectives must be to protect the client's brand and to convey the intended message. To do this, each component of the ad campaign must be accurately and consistently translated so that the consumer in the target market understands the message, recognizes it as part of a single, on-going campaign, and (ideally) finds it appealing. Utilizing the same highly experienced linguist(s), a comprehensive, up-to-date translation memory, and a formal in-country review by client representatives in the target market is the only way to ensure success.

Chapter 13: Case Studies

Product: Medical Device for the Home Consumer

Situation

Company Z recently developed a handheld device for the consumer market. The product analyzes and reports blood hormone levels to the user. Company Z just finished testing the English version of the device and is preparing for a simultaneous product launch in the US, Europe, and China.

We have twelve weeks before the product is scheduled for release at a product launch meeting with overseas sales and marketing staff.

Because the product is brand new, we assist Company Z in coordinating in-country review of the localization (by interfacing directly with their overseas market staff). Although twelve weeks is ample time for translation and testing, the project team must be well-organized and disciplined in developing terminology lists and executing in-country reviews of the materials.

Project Scope

User Interface:	1,200 words, in XML format, for Palm OS.
Help File:	5,500 words, delivered in Word format.
Quick Start Guide:	1,300 words in Quark format.
User Manual:	12,000 words in FrameMaker format.
Packaging materials:	500 words of packaging materials in Quark format.
Testing:	Functional testing of the UI on native operating systems required.
Timeline:	8 weeks for initial product localization, 2 weeks for localized product testing, followed by 2 weeks for in-country review and change implementation.

David Martin
Client Services Manager

Unlike the majority of my colleagues here at Lingo Systems, I don't speak a second language. That said, I love language. I studied English in college, dabbled in poetry, and taught English while a grad student at Virginia Tech. And along the way, I have always been interested in foreign cultures—the politics, the art, the style, the FOOD! I suppose it is appropriate, then, that my career path has led me to Lingo Systems.

Process

During the project scheduling and estimating process, Company Z and our localization team determine that, while our standard three-step translation process is more than adequate to meet timeline and quality expectations, the in-country review process presents some risks. Company Z does not have time available for the extensive fine tuning of the translations. However, Company Z has a strong reputation for quality in their foreign markets, so the product must be easy to use.

In order to maximize the quality of the translation and to remain within the agreed-upon timeline, we take steps to integrate Company Z's in-country review team early in the translation process. During the initial project kickoff, Company Z and the Lingo Systems project team review a list of expectations with each of Company Z's in-country reviewers. Their next involvement comes after we translate the product terminology list. We ask the in-country reviewers to review the translations and sign off on the terminology as appropriate. Our linguists then use the accepted terminology throughout the translation of the product. Following translation and testing of the UI, the in-country reviewer for each target language is provided with a demo of the translated product for final verification. Once approval is obtained, the translation team has one week to make any essential changes.

Product: SAP Implementation Training Program

Situation

A leading global manufacturer of consumer products recently acquired companies in the UK, France, Germany and the Netherlands. They decided to implement SAP to bring all the global businesses onto a common ERP platform. To maximize the utilization of the SAP system, a global end-user training program was initiated to accompany the implementation. After conducting an internal needs assessment, the company determined that the training would be more effective if taught in the native languages rather than English. Their training materials would therefore be needed in French, German, and Dutch in addition to English.

Chapter 13: Case Studies

The training materials included traditional instructor-led (ILT) materials, as well as a sophisticated web-based application that functioned as an intelligent help system sitting on top of SAP. The challenge was to find a localization partner who brought to the table experience with SAP, the ability to deliver quality results under aggressive timelines, and the technical know-how to work within the technical parameters of the project. Finally, and perhaps most importantly, the project budget was very limited, so the localization solution needed to be as cost-effective as possible—without compromising the need for quality and speed.

Project Scope

Database localization: 4 localizable tables in a SQL Server database, totaling 310,000 words.

Instructor Led Training: 30 PowerPoint presentations, totaling 1,350 slides and 65,000 words.

Supplemental Materials: 18 MS Word documents, totaling 85 pages and 11,000 words.

Timeline: 3 months.

Process

Given that the majority of the localizable content resided in an SQL Server database, extracting the text into a useable format for the linguistic tasks became a chief concern. Tables may be exported as Excel worksheets, however, there are notable disadvantages to using Excel. Field formatting is lost, and the management of string lengths becomes difficult if not impossible. Moreover, without the use of a sophisticated tool, repetitious strings cannot be excluded from the scope of work automatically.

Our solution was to select a globalization tool that was designed expressly for database localization (SQL Server, Access, Oracle, and others), providing an intuitive UI for the linguists, tools to manage string lengths, and the ability to identify and exclude duplicate strings from the scope of work. By excluding duplicate strings (repetitions) from the scope of the database translation and copy editing effort, we were able to significantly reduce the cost and timeline, as well as ensure that repetitions were translated consistently throughout. Because of the aggressive timeline required, we worked together with the client to prioritize the materials based on the training schedule. In this manner, we were able to customize a "just-in-time" localization process that functioned as a virtual assembly line, delivering materials to the customer as they were needed.

By using the right technology, the most qualified resources, and the optimum process, we were able to meet all of our client's requirements, helping them to maximize their substantial investment in SAP.

Product: Software with Multiple Versions

Situation

Company X is an industry leader in computer software applications for both businesses and consumers. Key products include a compression solution for multiple operating platforms and developer tools that focus on access management.

Three of Company X's largest overseas markets are Japan, Germany and France. Updated, localized versions of their software and support materials are released annually for these markets.

Before working with Lingo Systems, Company X used several vendors to translate their materials, each with a different localization process. Quality, consistency, and timelines varied significantly. It was determined that one vendor with a proven, well-documented localization process would improve consistency and quality. Moreover, by leveraging shared content, a single vendor would be able to lower overall costs.

Project Scope

User Interface:	132 rc files containing approximately 19,500 words.
Help Files: (Basic version)	8 HTML files containing approximately 3,500 words, 10 Screen captures and one localizable graphic.
Help Files: (Deluxe version)	131 HTML files containing approximately 39,000 words, 29 screen captures, and 21 localizable graphics.
User Guide:	1 FrameMaker document containing approximately 5,000 words and 10 screen captures.

Box Art: 1 InDesign document containing approximately 900 words, 5 screen captures, and 1 localizable graphic.

Timeline: 7 weeks

Process

After being selected as the new localization partner, Lingo Systems organized a conference call with Company X's product manager, localization manager and lead engineer to define the project scope, requirements, and milestones. Four areas of special attention were identified.

First, prior to starting the project, we evaluated the quality of previous translations and fixed them as necessary. Because our client had used multiple vendors, each working with their own translation memory, there were inconsistent translations and use of approved terminology. By performing a TM "clean up" we resolved these problems and created a solid foundation of quality translations from which to start the new project.

Second, to make the translations more consistent across all three product lines, we selected a lead linguist and a sole proofreader for each translating team. The lead linguist was tasked with supervising the translation and editing efforts to ensure consistent use of terminology and style. The proofreader performed the final review of all material so that a single person with an eye on the big picture could act as the gatekeeper for all translations. The combination of a solid TM, a single localization vendor, and a dedicated, organized translation team resulted in a much higher level of consistency across the three products.

Third, Company X asked us to localize the beta version of the software, Help, and documentation. We explained that this would likely result in numerous change orders for each component as new patches were incorporated (i.e., expensive and inefficient). Moreover, given that we would receive multiple drops of new strings and files, we determined that a hand-off tracking form would be necessary to organize and manage all of the requests and deliveries.

Finally, because Company X sells both a basic and deluxe version of the same software, two help systems were needed. Rather than translate both systems separately, we analyzed the content and found that the deluxe version already contained all of the help files for the basic version. By localizing the deluxe version first and then using the help authoring tool RoboHelp to isolate the individual topics that were part of the basic version, we were able to produce deliverables for both versions from a single set of translated files. Ultimately, this reduced the time required for translation and saved the company nearly $25,000.

Product: Heavy Equipment Operator Manual

Situation

AAA Cranes has been producing large construction cranes and similar equipment for over fifty years. They are known in their industry as a world-wide leader. For the past six years we have partnered with AAA to provide localized Operator Manuals for fifteen overseas markets. Because we have been creating and maintaining translation memories (TMs) for each target language over the years, AAA's localization costs are typically 1/3 of what they would be without these TMs. Also, because up to eighty percent of a given Operator Manual's content is shared with previously written manuals, the quality and consistency of the content is exemplary.

Project Scope

A typical AAA Crane manual is written using a standardized template in FrameMaker, is between 15,000 and 25,000 total words, and localized into fifteen languages.

Timeline: Because of the high leveraging across AAA Crane product documentation, we have been able to shave several weeks off of the normal translation process. Depending on the amount of leveraging available, we can deliver a 25,000-word manual in fifteen languages within five to seven weeks.

Process

In this case, our localization process has been modified to maximize the benefits of leveraging across the various products. We begin the project by reviewing the English master document in order to confirm that AAA's writers adhered to the style template. Following this review, we leverage the source text against our TMs by language. These pre-translated files are then forwarded to each target language translation team. Following translation of the new text and copy editing the new and leveraged text, the files are formatted, proofread, and put through our quality assurance (QA) review prior to delivery. Following delivery, we update each target language TM with the newly translated materials.

While all localization projects follow similar project process steps, each individual project presents an opportunity to adapt the localization process to precisely match desired outcomes. Each project is unique, so a cookie-cutter approach to localization does not work. The fundamentals, represented by the localization processes described in this book, must be malleable enough to meet the requirements for each client so that budget, timeline, and quality objectives are met.

Reebok introduced a women's running shoe called the Incubus - a name that refers to a mythological creature infamous for ravishing women while they sleep.

Paul Trotter
AuthorIT
Founder and CEO

Paul is the founder and CEO of AuthorIT Software Corporation, the makers of AuthorIT. Paul is also the architect of AuthorIT, and has been involved with documentation for over twelve years.

Chapter 14: Single-Source Content Management

by Paul Trotter

More and more businesses are expanding into international markets. A critical success factor for this expansion is high-quality, cost-effective, and timely translated written content. Responsibility for this typically falls on internal translation departments or localization partners. Translation comes at a high price, exceeding the cost of writing the original content after only a few languages.

Current approaches to localization rely on technologies and processes that have minimal scope for improvement. The localization industry is under increasing pressure to find new ways to improve cost-efficiency, quality, and time-to-market.

In this chapter I will try to explain what content management is and how it can help your organization more efficiently write higher quality and more effective documentation. I will also discuss how to re-use and share content across documents, have strict control over standards and branding, publish content to print, help, and Internet formats, and reduce the cost of localizing your content.

What is Content Management?

So what is content management? The first thing to say is that there is no single, agreed-upon definition. Content management is a relatively new discipline, and if you ask the many suppliers of content management software they all have different definitions. Of course, most of them make the definition suit what their software does.

It is fair to say that most people regard content management as applying solely or mainly to the management and delivery of web content. This is a very limited view. Content management software covers a much wider area, and can be categorized as follows:

- Web Content Management: This was the first and is the most common use of the term "content management." These systems are primarily used to help manage websites and web content. In this context the word "content" refers to any resource used to build a website. Most of these applications are only concerned with managing the delivery of the website. The authoring and maintenance are done by other products.

- Document/File Management: Document and file management systems are designed to manage whole documents and other files rather than the words and pictures inside them. They know little about what the files contain and treat them as just a "blob" of data. They rely heavily on users defining and applying metadata to give them more information. In practice, however, metadata is often not applied and the applications are little more than filing systems.
- Digital Asset Management: Very similar in nature to document and file management systems in that they manage files; but because they focus on multimedia there is little or no functionality for text intensive files. These applications are used mainly to create a central repository for graphics, video, flash, and other multimedia files, and provide archive, search, and retrieval functions.
- Source Control: Again similar to document and file management systems but they are primarily concerned with managing source code, which are pure text files. They usually have poor support for dealing with binary content and often provide integration with software development environments.
- Enterprise Content Management: This is one of the newest categories in content management and does not yet have a clear definition. Most providers in this space are actually combining many of the other categories and calling it "Enterprise" as it provides a wider scope.
- Single-Source Content Management: These systems provide the most benefits for localization. Rather than storing documents, they store and manage the content that is used to assemble those documents in small re-useable components. These components can be anything from a single word to many paragraphs or other components like graphics or links.

Single-source content management is an overall process for originating, managing, and publishing content right across the enterprise and to any output.

Content management should be an end-to-end solution providing the ability to track, manage, and control what happens to your content at all stages in the documentation cycle: from authoring and importing, to storage and document assembly, to multi-output publishing.

What is the Difference between Managing Content and Managing Files?

The answer to this question is the key to why single-source content management provides so many benefits over traditional file management systems.

The most important aspect to managing any kind of data is to control how it is created and changed. This is the cornerstone of enterprise applications of all types and is the only way you can truly manage information. The next step is adding value to it.

The typical approach to document and file management is to move the files from the file system into a database where they are stored in exactly the same format as they were created. These systems typically provide access control, versioning, metadata tagging, and search capabilities. There is little control, however, over the modification or creation of the files in the first place. Instead, they rely entirely on other applications to do that.

Let's look at this problem from a different perspective. Let's say your organization is using Excel spreadsheets to manage their financial accounts. At some point this approach becomes unmanageable for a variety of reasons. It is decided to move to a purpose-built accounting system that uses a backend database, allows multi-users, provides audit trails, has financial reporting, and is able to manage the underlying data.

Would you just move the Excel spreadsheets, as they are, into a file management system and expect it to magically create a profit and loss statement, or chart of accounts? Of course not, that would be impossible. Instead, you would move the data from the spreadsheets into the predefined relational database structure provided by the purpose-built accounting system. Now you would be able to get all your reporting, ensure data was entered correctly, have multiple users editing without fear of overwrites, and exercise a much greater degree of security over your data.

Would you expect to be able to continue editing your accounts in Excel? Of course not, the information is no longer in Excel format, and doing so would bypass your controls and auditing. You would now edit the information in a controlled fashion in the accounting system. No longer would you get an unbalanced transaction or have information changed by unauthorized sources. Best of all, your reporting is a mouse click away.

Single-source content management provides the same evolutionary leap for content. It provides a more effective and more efficient way of authoring, managing, publishing and localizing your organization's documents, images, web content, etc.

Why Do You Need Content Management?

Content is an Asset

Generating content takes time and money—often lots of both. So content should be treated as the valuable asset that it is.

To get maximum value from your documentation resources, you should be able to do a number of things:

- Re-use content across documents without copying so that you can write it once and maintain it in a single place, no matter how many times you have used it.
- Use content created for one purpose equally well in other contexts and for other purposes.
- Translate re-used content once and have it automatically reflected wherever it is used.
- Publish to print, help, and Internet outputs without having to modify or make different versions of your content.
- Involve more people in the documentation process, such as subject matter experts, application developers, localization teams, and trainers.

These features have the potential for increasing the quality and consistency of your documentation, reducing the cost and time involved in producing it, and gaining more value from every piece of content that you create.

Control is Essential

Assets are of no use if you can't manage them. Having a large amount of content that you can't find, organize, protect, or use effectively is simply a waste of time.

Involving more people is a good idea, but it requires serious organization. Wider access can be a disaster if the system can't cope.

To properly control your content, you must be able to:

- Set and enforce your standards to ensure consistency and quality,
- Control who in the organization can create, see, and use content,
- Find the content components when you need them,
- Manage the content lifecycle through drafts, reviews, localization, release, and archiving, and
- Control what can be published to each output channel and by whom.

What are the Savings and Benefits?

An Example of Cost Savings

Whether you choose to manage the translation in-house or to outsource it to an external vendor, localization can be a complicated and expensive process. On the first mention of localization the immediate reaction from your financial department may be to reach defensively for their wallets. Costs can be unpredictable and can quickly get out of control, particularly if you don't know what to expect. Let's look at an example to put this in perspective:

The average cost that a translator will charge varies significantly, but for illustration purposes, assume a rate of 25 cents (US) per word. Take a document with 500 pages and an average of 200 words per page. That's 100,000 words so you're quickly looking at $25,000.

Now remember that's just for the initial translation. There will be more costs when you make modifications to the original document and need it retranslated. Most translation agencies use translation memory tools which help reduce the effort involved in retranslating a document, but they still charge for the whole document (albeit at a reduced word rate for the text already translated).

Chapter 14: Content Management

When using translation memory tools, a *fuzzy match* is returned when a text segment is similar but not identical. An *exact match* (100%) is returned when there is no difference or variation between the two segments. Translators often charge different rates for exact matches, fuzzy matches (with the match falling between a certain percentage), or new, previously untranslated text.

Let's get back to our example. You now modify five percent of these pages, and add twenty new pages. Without allowing for fuzzy matches, the cost of retranslation can quickly approach $10,000:

20 new pages - 4,000 words @ 25 cent per word	$1,000
5% change - 5,000 words @ 25 cents per word	$1,250
95% unchanged - topics with 95,000 words @ 8 cents	$7,600
Total cost of update	**$9,850**

Over time, these costs quickly mount up. Our example was just one document into one language. Translate that same document into ten other languages, and multiply the cost ten times. Translate a further ten or one hundred documents into multiple languages, and watch your costs skyrocket!

How Single-source Content Management Reduces Translation Costs:

- Using a content management system that stores and manages content in XML format can facilitate localization. It can also yield significant savings.
- You only translate objects that have been modified.

  For example, let's go back to our five hundred page document which we've now updated. Rather than sending the translator all five hundred pages again, only the twenty new pages and the five percent of modified pages are exported as XML. Using our previous example this would reduce the cost of retranslation from $9,850 to $2,250!

- Text is only translated once. The same components are reused in multiple documents. For example, the same copyright notice (or even an entire introductory chapter) may be used over and over. Each component only requires translation once. You can even reuse content as small as a phrase, sentence, or paragraph which takes reuse even further, and again, only pay for translation once.

- Cross references and hyperlinks don't require translation. Because they are inserted at publishing time, taking their text from the heading of the component they reference, they aren't stored in the text, resulting in less to translate. Likewise, reference text such as *See* and *on Page* is defined by templates, so only the template requires translation.

The Guide to Translation and Localization

- Our studies have shown an average *thirty percent reduction in word count* through reuse of content.
- The XML files do not contain formatting.

  When the same text string is found using different character formatting, translation memory tools do not always identify it as an exact match. Because the XML files in a content management tool do not contain formatting, this helps increase the exact matches found.

Benefits of Localization

When you manage your content at a more granular level there are a number of things you can do that cannot be done with whole documents. Some of the specific benefits of localization are:

- Translate Content Once: The system knows what content is translatable, has been previously translated, is reused, or has been added or changed since the last translation. Only content that actually requires translation is sent to translators, which significantly reduces word count and cost of translation.
- Faster Time to Market: Localization and content creation can run in tandem, allowing translation to finish much sooner. Content is created in small discrete components that can immediately be sent for translation. This avoids the costly exercise of translating drafts or waiting for completion of the entire source content.
- Automated Single-source Publishing: Once source content is translated and reviewed, it can be published directly to print, help, and Internet formats without tweaking or rework. This provides substantial savings, and eliminates inconsistencies in translation across delivery formats.
- Cleaner Translation Memory: Translatable XML contains only text and semantic markup, increasing translation memory accuracy, and eliminating the effect of formatting codes on matches in the memory.
- Improved Accountability: Only content that requires translation is sent for translation. Each piece of content has an accurate word count and is known by all parties in the process, avoiding any surprises or disputes.

Overall Benefits of Content Management

Single-source content management provides significant benefits and cost savings over traditional document authoring and maintenance methods. Some of these are:

- Faster Time to Market: Because authors spend far less time creating and recreating the same content, reviewers spend less time reviewing and translators spend less time translating. Publishing to print, help, and Internet formats is fully automated.

Chapter 14: Content Management

This is achieved by controlling standards, eliminating duplication, and effectively managing creation, localization, and publishing of content.

- Efficient Use of Resources: By eliminating repetitive creation and maintenance, more of your resources can be devoted to improving the quality of the content and adding value to your documentation. Many clients report savings in excess of twenty percent through reuse of content.
- Major Production Cost Savings: Efficient creation, maintenance, and management of content will naturally result in major cost savings. You achieve more documentation for less outlay and the time taken to produce a page through traditional authoring tools can be halved.
- Lower Translation Costs: Content is translated only once no matter how often it is reused. Translators only ever work on new or changed source content, so you don't pay for them to handle unchanged text. Real projects have shown reductions in translation word count in excess of thirty percent.
- Improved Quality and Usability of Content: Through enforcement of standards you can guarantee consistent documentation structure and formatting, increasing readability and usability. Using single-source content ensures one hundred percent consistency wherever it appears.
- Improved Workplace Satisfaction: Freeing authors from tedious, time-consuming tasks such as formatting and repetitive updates allows them to concentrate on creating and improving content. Reviewers gain by reviewing content only once, regardless of the number of end deliverables. Writers save ninety-five percent of the time they usually spend formatting content.
- Increased Customer Satisfaction: Consistent, accurate documentation of all types means fewer calls to customer support because you are providing the right information, at the right time, in the right format.

About AuthorIT

AuthorIT is the new breed in content management tools for authoring, management, and publishing of printed and online documentation. AuthorIT solves the documentation problem by addressing the cause, not by attempting to treat the symptoms. AuthorIT is truly single-source, allowing you to utilize single-source authoring, single-source collaboration, and single-source publishing. AuthorIT is currently used in over fifty countries across five continents. For more information, see **www.author-it.com**.

Chapter 15: But They Speak English, Right?

by Perry Brooks

Perry Brooks
Brandfluency
Localization Director

English grammar never really made sense to me until I began studying other languages, but I grew up in Arkansas, so that shouldn't be much of a surprise. And I'm probably the only Southerner who hates cornbread.

Global Branding Solutions

World-class brands don't just stop at the border—that's merely where they begin. Extending brands across other languages is much more than simply retrofitting translated text into an existing layout using the usual desktop publishing (DTP) applications. Rather, it is making sure that the overall brand experience itself is maintained and correctly conveyed in the new target languages and cultures.

In other words, how does the overall brand (its messaging and core values, along with readily identifiable graphic components such as logos, typefaces, images, colors and artwork) express itself after making the jump from, say, English to Arabic?

At Brandfluency, our goal is to ensure that a brand's core elements and values aren't diluted or lost in translation. When done properly, brand localization ensures that:

- The brand's look and feel stays the same, regardless of language or writing system used, and more importantly,
- The final component feels natural and appropriate to the target culture, as if it were created expressly for them in their own country by a native speaker.

Ask yourself, is your brand going places...and can it get there more efficiently?

In the past, our large domestic market and homogeneous language demographic have allowed many American companies to focus exclusively on the US domestic market, resulting in an overwhelmingly domestic mindset when it comes to brands and products.

This cultural and linguistic insulation has put many companies at a disadvantage when entering overseas markets, and there have been some particularly famous examples of American companies' cultural gaffes documented in this book. Europe has been ahead of the global branding curve for decades when it comes to brand localization, due to so many language markets in close geographic proximity. Several

Chapter 15: Global Branding

of the countries are officially bilingual (e.g., Belgium, Finland), others unofficially multilingual (e.g., Spanish, Catalan, Basque and Galician in Spain), and one even quadrilingual (French, Spanish, Italian and Romansch in Switzerland). The latter is sufficient to make most American marketing departments faint.

But in today's interconnected global marketplace, many well-known American corporations now see sixty to seventy percent of their revenue coming from abroad, and must start taking other target languages and cultures into account during product and brand development.

Even the US is no longer a monolingual country. America now has more Spanish speakers than the entire population of Canada, making English-only brand decisions no longer a viable option, and leaving many companies puzzled—exactly how do they get started putting a global face on their brands?

It's a daunting task, and rightly so: localizing any product is frequently a complex process, and that process can be further complicated when brand identity enters the equation. Typically, branding and related creative services are outsourced to a creative design agency. Most design firms don't have the experience, background, or specialized software needed to work with non-Latin-based languages. And many advertising agencies have little experience (or confidence) working with copy in languages other than English.

To successfully localize branded products you should consider contracting an experienced, global brand management resource with multilanguage and multicultural capabilities. Such a firm will be able to navigate and sort out the myriad issues encountered when introducing brands and print-focused collateral to new markets.

Often, a global branding initiative begins with analysis and planning for product packaging. In the world of branding, packaging is an environment in which presentation is as important as content. The same stringent brand standards used for English packaging must be maintained across all other language versions. In order to bridge the gap between global design and localization requirements, you'll want to select a team that brings branding sensibility, attention to detail, multilingual capability, and the latest in technology to high-end print production.

Only a very few agencies have the experience and proven methodology to combine all of these skills. The benefits, however, can be huge. By consolidating functions with one vendor, the resulting advantages will include:

- Immediate saving from lower direct costs,
- Faster time to market,
- Accelerated revenue stream,
- Improved communication, coordination, and workflow,
- Reduced vendor and project management costs,
- Consistent branding, appearance, terminology and message across all language versions,
- Higher quality and consistency, and
- Allows you to focus on your core competency and your vendor to focus on theirs.

So, how do we begin a global brand initiative? At the most basic level, we start by asking a lot of questions. Frequently our role becomes not only brand steward, but also auditor, serving as a sort of third-party mediator throughout the process of brand localization and implementation, often asking and clarifying nagging brand issues that may have lingered unanswered for years.

Working with our client and their various teams to better understand the brand, we recommend starting with the establishment of brand standards, then standardizing a brand's components, such as typefaces, logos, artwork and copy. After the brand components have been solidified, we proceed with implementation, template creation, production, prepress and ultimately rollout of the new campaign.

Something as rudimentary as text handling can often become a major obstacle to starting projects in other languages. At Brandfluency, our workstations can handle a number of languages—from common ones such as German, to more complicated writing systems, like Japanese, Arabic, or even Hindi—allowing us to fluidly work across language versions, removing the more technical aspects and improving consistency. To help streamline the process, we've also compiled an arsenal of best practices, which include a number of processes, automation, font technologies, and both XML and PDF-based workflows, gleaned by actual project work, winnowing out what works from what doesn't.

While no two brands are alike, neither are the processes to localize them, although there are some important things companies should keep in mind when starting a brand localization:

- Localization cannot be an afterthought. It must be an integral part of the entire development process. Start with the design and concepting phases, and think about how a particular design or artwork would work when paired with different writing systems or cultures.

- Brand localization is an art and not a conversion.
- Plan accordingly for localization during schedule development—a tagline or crucial marketing copy that takes months to craft in English cannot be expected to be translated in several hours.
- Ask many questions, and make no assumptions. If you don't know whether the French for a project should be European or Canadian, don't guess. Take the time to find out.
- Keep in mind when given something to review, everyone is an editor, and international subsidiaries may want changes made to the translated copy. It's a natural part of the process. After all, when was the last time your company agreed on a new slogan without several rounds of revisions?
- Solicit feedback. Foreign subsidiaries can sometimes provide the best perspective from the field on how to approach messaging for a particular country. For example, is borderless brand messaging appropriate for your company, or would a varied regional approach be a better fit?

Ultimately, the most important thing is the brand experience itself, which should resonate regardless of the target language or culture used to convey it. Companies should never lose sight of this, because in this day and age not only do brands travel the globe more readily than people—but with equally good products competing in virtually every category, it's frequently the brand experience that drives consumer choice.

About Brandfluency^{SM}

Brandfluency^{SM}, a specialty group of Seven Worldwide, is a team of brand, localization, and print professionals who understand how to leverage a brand identity into any one of over seventy languages, while making sure the message isn't diluted or lost in translation.

With us, brands don't just stop at the border—that's merely where they begin.

Our integrated linguistic and production professionals can put together an efficient localization solution that meets your requirements, whether you need help with a major international print campaign or initial consultation to help you over a rough spot in your global design, planning, or implementation process.

Ask yourself, is your brand going places...and can it get there more efficiently? For more information, see **www.brandfluency.com**.

Chapter 16: Testing and Integration of Software and Hardware

Wasi Wahedi
PCTest
CEO

Being raised in Afghanistan and participating in the resistance movement before coming to the US has given me a tremendous appreciation of the freedom and choices available in the United States. Not only the choices of education and career opportunities, but also the freedom to enjoy recreational activities. I only wish I had more time to travel and see the world, my enduring passion.

by Wasi Wahedi

Whether you are releasing a computer game, income tax software, a complicated business enterprise solution, a children's toy that interfaces to a computer, or any other technology product, it has to be thoroughly tested before being released to market. You don't want your customer to spend hours in frustration pouring over their new product, or on endless calls with your customer support department. Not only will you lose an opportunity to establish product loyalty with the customer, but dealing with such problems is both expensive and unproductive.

A third party testing and integration provider can play a key role in the product development lifecycle. Pre-release product testing and quality assurance is a critical part of any technology product release. Whether this step is performed by in-house resources or is outsourced to a testing company, there are many types of tests that can and should be performed to ensure the product functions as intended.

If you choose to outsource, the testing and integration provider will most likely have a basic testing model that can be easily modified depending on whether they are testing a software program or a digital device, and depending on the degree and scope of changes being made. Multilanguage testing may require further customization to allow for cultural and linguistic differences, as well as internationalization issues. For instance a tax program for the United Kingdom would be substantially different from a tax program in the US, with entirely different functionality—and different outputs. Even products as simple as toys may differ from one cultural base to another, so great care must be taken to ensure that these differences are appropriately tested and localized.

Each testing vendor may have slightly, or even radically different approaches to test planning and execution. At PCTest, our testing model has four basic phases. Not every phase will be needed on every project. Moreover, products that contain major changes to only one process, or minimal changes to a few processes/applications, may be candidates for combining test phases. In all cases, however, a comprehensive test plan must be prepared and approved prior to any work being performed. Once the project does begin, it does not proceed to the next phase of testing until specific release criteria have been met for the current phase.

Chapter 16: Testing & Integration

Unit Test

Unit testing is the first phase of product testing, and is intended to be the lowest level and most detailed test phase. PCTest has defined two levels of unit testing.

Level I Unit Test

Level I unit testing is conducted by the client's development staff during the coding phase and is intended to ensure that changes are working at a load module level as outlined in the business requirements. The developer focuses on functional, navigational, and logic testing:

- Every major program branch executed at least once,
- Boundary conditions checked on all major branches; such as greater than, equal to, and less than cases,
- Minimum and maximum limits just reached, and then exceeded,
- Initialization logic exercised,
- First and last record on file processed, and
- Empty file encountered.

For online programs:

- All edit conditions violated,
- All screen flow branches taken, and
- All function keys used.

For reports, all the following are carefully checked:

- Headings,
- Page breaks,
- Totals and subtotals, and
- Format of all fields.

The Guide to Translation and Localization

Level II Unit Test—Informal Integration

Level II unit testing consists of an informal integration test of all *load modules* for the product, and is normally conducted by a testing and integration specialist such as PCTest. Our analyst verifies that abbreviated logic changes work with other pieces of the product, verifies functionality, and executes a limited regression test. The tracking of incidents begins with this phase of testing.

User Requirements Verification Test

Client representatives (typically end users) conduct user requirements tests to ensure that the developer has captured all business requirements in the coding changes. Prior to moving to the next phase of testing, the project sponsor must review the changes and agree that the developer met business requirements as submitted. There is no testing for bugs in this phase. Additionally, this is not an opportunity to add new enhancements or make major changes to requirements outside the scope of the original system documentation.

Systems Integration/Regression Tests

A designated tester or test team conducts systems integration tests. This phase of testing incorporates logic, functional, and regression tests of all requirements from a technical perspective. The objective is to verify that changes or enhancements do not adversely affect pre-existing functionality and interfaces to other products or systems. Testing companies such as PCTest are ideally equipped to perform integration and regression tests.

Chapter 16: Testing & Integration

Final User Acceptance/Regression Test

The final phase of testing is often referred to as Beta testing, production review, or, in some cases, a pilot phase. Beta testing ensures that the various integrated components match, operate with, and/or communicate with each other. The objective of final user acceptance testing is to complete logic, functional, and regression tests to confirm that changes are in accordance with the business requirements and that they have not negatively impacted the business process and/or production environment in any way. The testing process utilized for this phase of testing should emulate the business process in the business unit (i.e., emulate a real world scenario).

The business sponsors requesting/supporting changes are responsible for the verification and acceptance of all changes. They are also required to formally approve the acceptance.

Localization Testing

The above discussion covers the basic testing model that would be appropriate for most hardware and software applications. For global releases, the application may be translated into other languages in order to reach consumers in those countries. In this instance, the testing plan will also need to incorporate localization testing to ensure that the translated versions function properly in each native language, that there are no unique problems to that environment or language, and that it is user-friendly in every language. In many cases, this testing will also need to be performed on native operating systems (e.g., a German version of Windows).

There are many other tests that can be performed by a testing company to ensure your product is ready for the global marketplace. Applications or products that are released in more than one language should be tested in each language on native systems to ensure full functionality.

Accessibility Testing

Accessibility testing is used to identify and resolve functionality and usability limitations within websites and products that would otherwise prevent disabled people from using the technologies to their maximum advantage. Resolving these problems fulfills legal obligations and provides assurance that your product will be accessible by the widest possible audience.

Benchmark Testing

Benchmark testing is used to measure the performance of your hardware, software, Internet application, or other product against some standard of excellence or achievement by identifying the measurable successes of others and applying them to your own organization.

Competitive Analysis

Competitive analysis is a process by which detailed information on functionality is gathered on a competitor's company, device, or product for the sake of understanding and for future product development.

Interoperability Testing

Interoperability testing ensures that two or more systems (computers, communication devices, networks, software, and other information technology components) are able to interact with one another and exchange data according to a prescribed method in order to achieve predictable results.

Load Testing

Load testing (sometimes called volume testing or performance engineering) determines how an application deals with large tasks. Stress testing examines application behavior under peak bursts of activity.

OEM Product Validation

Frequently, an OEM company differentiates itself from its suppliers by adding unique features to generic products. OEM validation testing verifies product claims and validates added features.

Performance Testing

Performance testing focuses on how web applications function under real world loads and connectivity, and includes the interaction of customers, web applications, and the Internet.

Sustaining Testing

Sustaining testing is similar to acceptance testing in that it is done on a percentage of randomly-selected units off the production line. Unlike acceptance testing, which is based on a customer's requirements and is generally non-destructive, sustaining testing is aimed at catching problems that may creep in due to design changes and often includes the same tests (including destructive tests) used during qualification testing.

Usability Testing

Usability testing is similar to verification testing except that it is performed throughout the production cycle and usually includes only three evaluators.

Verification Testing

Verification testing is executed at the end of the production cycle when functionality of the product is at or close to one hundred percent completed. Typically, the testing is extensive, and consists of areas such as usefulness, effectiveness, learnability, and likeability. Each test requires as many as one hundred evaluators of varying skill levels and includes interviews before, during, and after evaluation.

About PCTest

PCTest provides enterprise-wide testing services for hardware, software, and web/e-commerce applications. The company's state of the art testing lab is unrivalled in the Pacific Northwest. With a rolling inventory of more than 1,000 computers, PCTest can provide large scale network testing for any size client or system configuration. Core testing solutions include:

- Compatibility
- Accessibility
- Functionality
- Load and Stress
- Benchmarking
- Performance

PCTest also offers a comprehensive outsourcing solution to supplement or replace in-house resources, providing greater capacity at a lower cost. Since its founding in 1991, the Company has tested more than 4,000 products. Clients include educational companies, toy companies, shrink-wrapped software companies, medical device companies, and service companies. For more information, see **www.pctest.com**.

Chapter 17: Cultural Training and Awareness

by Danielle Walker

Danielle Walker
Training Management Corporation
President and CEO

Over the past 20 years, Ms. Walker has worked and consulted extensively with major corporations in North America, Asia, Europe and the Middle East. A native of Morocco, she is fluent in French, English, Hebrew and Magrebian Arabic. She is also an author of the *Doing Business Globally* (1995, 2003) and the *Doing Business Internationally* series, including the *Guide to Cross-Cultural Success, A Self-Instructional Workbook, The Resource Book, Doing Business in Countries/Regions*, and *Managing Across Cultures*.

Introduction

Organizations everywhere must contend with numerous issues that affect their marketplace, workforce and operations. These challenges multiply when companies consider expanding globally. To improve the likelihood of success, many global organizations have launched initiatives to raise the cultural awareness of their employees and managers, and to equip them with the requisite mind and skill sets to adapt their business systems, processes and practices.

An effective cultural training program should begin with a reliable assessment of an individual's cultural awareness and preferences. From there, programs can be tailored to build effective skills and provide behavioral adaptations for multicultural management teams engaged in global business.

There are three broad and compelling imperatives for launching a cultural awareness and training initiative:

Global Business Performance: The global marketplace is diverse, giving organizations access to a broad spectrum of knowledge, talent and markets. When managed well, this diversity grows into a cultural asset, improving innovation, time to market, productivity, customer/client relations and, therefore, the financial bottom line.

Corporate Citizenship: To cultivate customer and employee loyalty and to ensure lasting success in local markets, international enterprises have to prove themselves to be valuable contributors to the communities within which they operate. Integrity in values and the relentless exercise of social and environmental responsibility are important investments for the long-term viability and growth of the business.

Growing Anti-Discrimination Legislation: Currently, sixty-eight countries have adopted anti-discrimination legislation, with twenty-five monitoring compliance. These countries are part of a growing trend focused on providing equitable access to employment and economic opportunity. For organizations this means more than legal compliance; those that embrace the trend can tap into dormant talent, resources and markets inaccessible to others.

Chapter 17: Cultural Training

About Culture

At TMC, we believe that most approaches to cultural awareness fall short and are not well matched to the types of challenges typically faced by globalizing organizations and by global managers and leaders. To be useful, such programs need to be of practical value in helping us to (1) navigate a broad spectrum of differences, (2) understand the fundamentals of various cultures and cross-cultural interactions and (3) translate this understanding into personal behaviors and organizational expectations. To guide us in our endeavor, we have developed several axioms about culture:

Axiom 1: Cultural Boundaries Are Not National Boundaries

In the field of cross-cultural communication, the concept of cultural boundaries is often used interchangeably with those of geographical and political boundaries (i.e., the nation). This perspective delineates different values and belief systems largely on the basis of national boundaries and nicely matches the contemporary understanding of the world, in which we have institutionalized the boundaries of sovereign nation-states as the universally recognized boundaries between peoples.

This notion has served well those businesses that divided the world into neat geographic regions and serviced them with a multinational organizational structure. However, with the dynamic expansion of globalization, using geographical/political worldviews to represent cultural differences is no longer useful and in fact carries with it rather dangerous baggage.

The habit of attributing characteristics to nationally defined groups is both unrealistic and unproductive in the global work environment. First, less than ten percent of the world's nation-states can be considered homogeneous. In only half of these nation-states is there a single ethnic group that makes up more than seventy-five percent of the population. Multiculturalism is surely the norm and cultural homogeneity the exception.

Axiom 2: Culture Is A Shared Pattern of Ideas, Emotions and Behaviors

Culture operates on both a conscious and unconscious level; it is both a characteristic of groups and is carried by individuals. Many of the commonly used definitions of culture highlight these features.

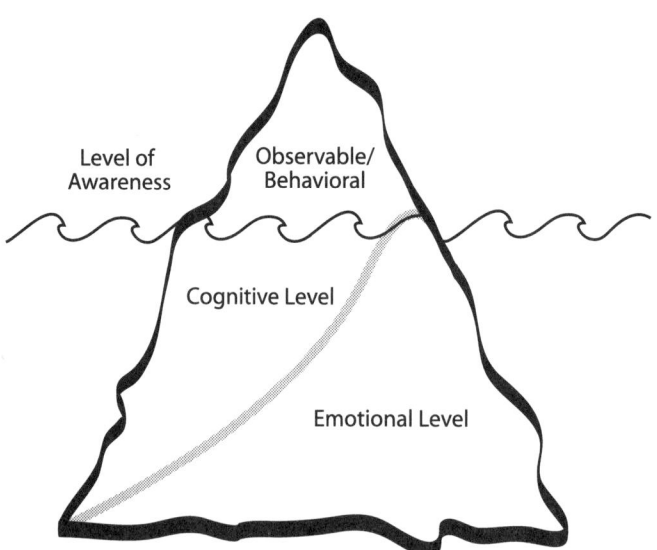

We suggest that it is useful, in attempting to understand the programming language of culture, to think of it as an iceberg. The proverbial "tip of the iceberg" symbolizes the level of behavior and other observables/tangibles—i.e., the world of manifestations. Beneath the level of our daily awareness, this behavior is linked to a world of values and meaning that is shared by a group. This internal world, which consists of ideas and their emotional value, is symbolically expressed as the "bottom of the iceberg."

In simplistic terms, the shared linkage between a behavioral expression (a handshake or a bow) and an idea or notion constitutes a norm. If we observe, for example, that a particular group of people tends to shake hands upon meeting, we may call this behavior the social norm for this group. The shared linkage between an idea/notion and an emotion can be considered a value.

It is important to recognize the connection between norms and values by defining culture as the complex pattern of ideas, emotions and observable/symbolic manifestations (including behaviors, practices, institutions and artifacts) that tends to be expected, reinforced and rewarded by and within a particular group.

Axiom 3: Cultures Reflect Distinctive Value Orientations at Various Levels

We may describe culture as holographic. Holographic images are built in such a way that the smallest part contains the entirety of the image. The magnificence of the entire three-dimensional image that we behold is the result of the amplification and magnification of the totality of the smallest parts. Culture seems to work in much the same way in that its smallest part, namely the individual, contains within it the deep structure of values and norms. Both are amplified and reinforced in interpersonal interactions. The small group or, in a business context, the team further magnifies and reinforces cultural configurations. The same thing happens again at the larger societal level or, in a business context, at the organizational level.

It is useful to distinguish four interrelated levels of culture:

1. *The individual, interpersonal level.* This level is the primary building block of culture. It is at this level that we most significantly experience and create culture, specifically through and in interactions with others. We may think of ourselves as reflections of a societal pattern of values and norms, a reflection that we exhibit through our actions and interactions. Through ourselves, we can both become aware of the larger societal patterns and also affect cultural changes through active shifts and changes in these patterns.

2. *The group or team level.* This level refers to social groupings of varying sizes as well as to functional/professional groups and teams. Each such group requires a set of values and norms if it is to be cohesive. As our interactions shape the dynamics of the group or team of which we are members, we as individuals directly affect the pattern of values and norms that define that group or team.

3. *The organizational level.* This level is a further amplification of basic cultural themes and configurations. It represents the deep patterns of values and norms that define societal institutions, including business organizations.

4. *The societal level.* This level involves the distinctive set of values, norms, practices and institutions that define what it means to be a member of the society. It is the largest frame in which we feel membership, such as the nation or modern society.

Summary

When organizations globalize, the skill base of every manager changes and the importance of cultural awareness becomes increasingly important. Every cultural group is characterized by a distinct set of behavioral norms, practices and institutions. An effective training and awareness program will embrace these differences and improve the ability of individuals, teams and organizations to perform across a broad cultural spectrum. Most importantly, it will also enable individuals and groups to contribute to their fullest potential by leveraging their unique experiences, perspectives and viewpoints for the collective benefit of all stakeholders.

About TMC

TMC provides learning and consulting solutions that ensure organizations, teams, and individuals attain the cultural agility required to compete globally. These custom learning solutions are distinguished by their cross-cultural perspective and are attuned to the realities of large, complex organizations. They include classroom, internet-based, and knowledge-on-demand training in several key areas:

- Global Management and Leadership
- Global Diversity/Inclusive Leadership
- Cross-Cultural Awareness and Management
- Multicultural Team Development
- Change Management and Organizational Alignment for Effective Globalization

TMC's global competencies will empower your organization to develop an effective multicultural workforce, increase managerial competencies, adapt sales and marketing practices to multicultural groups, and convert cultural differences to cultural assets. For more information, see **www.tmcorp.com**.

Chapter 18: Translation and Localization Today, Tomorrow, and the Day After

by Laurel Wagers

Laurel Wagers
MultiLingual Computing, Inc.
Managing Editor

I have a four-foot shelf of language books at home. They're fascinating. Unfortunately, owning them has not been enough to make me multilingual. But in working at the intersection of language and technology, I learn something every day. And that's fun.

In this book, the experienced translators and localizers at Lingo Systems have described the state of their art. They've shown how a client can prepare for a language project, what happens when that preparation is done right, and what happens when it's done poorly. They've shared their experiences in this challenging field, and they've generously given their potential clients the tools they need to plan, conduct, and evaluate a project. This is valuable stuff, solid information that can remove hesitation, clear up uncertainty, and provide a foundation for successful business efforts.

But it's all subject to change. In the fifteen years that MultiLingual Computing, Inc., has existed, even in the mere six years I've been part of it, language technology has changed enormously. The early call for multiple-language support in major operating systems has been met; fonts are available that include all the 65,000-plus characters in the Unicode encoding scheme; the PDF format with embedded fonts has made multilingual documents and websites not only possible but practicable. Windows, Macintosh and Linux users all have the tools to work in the world's major languages and scripts, as well as many that are less commonly used. Translation tools are developing in a variety of ways to keep up with the constantly increasing flood of information being shipped around the world in increasingly varied formats. Internationalization and support of multiple languages are no longer "nice to have" software options, but necessities. Many clients require these technologies, and if the major software companies don't provide versions for their languages, independent developers will. The next step is for multilingualism to become a *given*, a quality that is assumed; and a product will be considered deficient without it.

Chapter 18: The Future

The fundamentals of transferring information and ideas from one language to another are simple. One person speaks or writes in his or her language of choice; that person or someone else interprets or translates the information into another language; and another person hears or reads the interpreted/translated text. Then that person receives and responds to the information—and, one hopes, understands it. This much stays the same. How that translation takes place, however, is changing rapidly, as this Guide has made clear.

For many years, the principal translation tools were a dictionary, a writing instrument and paper (or papyrus or vellum). The typewriter and then the computer changed a translator's output method. Receiving the project in the form of computer files and working with the files introduce a number of new elements in the workflow. Translation memory allows even a pen-and-paper translator to look back at a database of previous work and improve the quality of his or her input as well. Now, using web-based tools and exchange formats, translators can collaborate on global projects without leaving their offices or buying new software. The translator is often called on to work with machine translation software that "pretranslates" text before it reaches him or her, and the translator's role sometimes becomes that of post-editor. All this changes the specific steps in the process and may increase a translator's speed, but does not alter the time-honored flow: source-language text > expert translator + currently available tools > target-language text.

One trend at present is the commodification of translation—considering translation a mere product or a standardized component of a project. Translation and localization of even the most complex software products and websites typically cost a fraction of one percent of the total being spent. Decision makers who understand language issues know that language quality is worth the investment; good localization typically results in revenue increases many times greater than the cost of the work. But clients looking for cost savings may issue quote requests that emphasize price above other factors. If language is a commodity, and if quality is irrelevant or actually can be standardized, then perhaps price is a major factor. But neither a skilled human translator nor translation software comes absolutely free. The free translations available online, for example, will produce words—but a "gist translation" at best. The translation engine won't fit those literally translated words into a particular business or social context. It can't understand or convey emphasis, humor, personal style. The customer gets what he or she pays for—and perhaps a place on the latest Internet list of translation gaffes.

Chapter 18: The Future

Another development that will affect translation and localization is a convergence of technologies, whether that means combining phone and Internet in one device, linking records systems on the Internet, or being able to talk to a "smart" house or car. Markup languages and exchange formats such as HTML, XML, SGML, TMX; the "metalanguage" of the Semantic Internet that specifies relations of words and concepts; the users' desire for combined functions in communication devices—all of these are changing the way people connect with one another. It's even been described as a move toward a "global mind" that not only contains immense amounts of information but, as programs "learn" to read and write to one another, that global electronic mind will be able to analyze, sift, and recombine information on its own—in any language.

On the one-to-one level, personal translators may make on-the-spot interpretation a matter of technology. Some such speech-to-speech devices are in development and even in use by military forces; versions for personal civilian use are emerging. The Star Trek universal translator is not just science fiction: it is in development.

Only a few years into the cell-phone/pager/SMS evolution, we can see how day-to-day communication is changing on a personal level. Increasingly sophisticated language technology is embedded in our lives. With multimedia messaging and—tomorrow, if not today—instant multilingual multimedia messaging, kids in Portland, Oregon, will be chatting with their friends in St. Petersburg, Russia, sending video messages in English that will be received in Russian; the reply, sent in Russian, will be received in English. And they will not find it remarkable that they can do this.

In Europe, with 21 official languages in the European Union (EU) and dozens more unofficial languages all around the continent, translation is a major part of the EU budget. Recently, when the flood of documentation rose too high, the EU decreed not that it had to find more translators or that the existing translators had to work harder, but that the documents had to be shorter and clearer. Translators will work through pivot languages-Estonian to French, or English to Greek, for example, rather than directly between Estonian and Greek.

The Guide to Translation and Localization

A related, important aspect of dealing with the massive amount of documentation to be translated in the public and private spheres is writing with translation in mind. Writing for translation is a concept that technical writers and translators—separately, at least—both consider of enormous importance. In a recent MultiLingual Computing survey, the tradition of "throwing a project over the wall" from source-language writers and production team to translators and localizers was one of the greatest frustrations identified by professionals on both sides of the wall. Documentation that is hard to understand in one language is not likely to be improved by a faithful translation into another. Controlled language, collaboration and the use of ever-more-sophisticated translation tools to process the source-language content are possible solutions. All these possibilities are ways and means toward the same end: clear and useful documents in many languages.

How will the translation-localization-internationalization-globalization industry change and develop? In many ways and directions, I think, as individual translators and companies face change and incorporate technology that suits their special situations. The individual translator with pen, paper, and dictionary will always have a place however much the language industry changes, because high-tech solutions are not suitable for every translation. Translators will continue to work with all the tools available, such as translation memory, which reduces repetitive work; content management and workflow technologies, which help organize large projects; and speech-to-text, which helps its user to produce documents with less physical effort.

Mergers, acquisition, and consolidation have been part of the translation and localization industry, but bigness has its own limitations; small companies and independent translators have their strengths. Innovation and niche specialization will continue as well.

Some people in the industry use the acronym GILT (globalization, internationalization, localization, translation). Unfortunately, when I see the word gilt, I think of surface embellishment, a thin layer of gold over something less valuable. In the world marketplace, whether the product is software or sofa cushions, a technical manual or a famine-relief organization's website, multilingual presentation and multilingual support are not *gilt* at all. They are essential components. And just as the developer would not hand responsibility for accounting support or website design to just anyone, neither should developers, manufacturers, or marketers require, expect, accept, or settle for less than thoroughly professional language work where clear communication is needed.

This means trained people with top-notch, up-to-date language skills; with technical expertise in the handling of language tools; and with a commitment to excellence in their work. The client is unlikely to know all the languages of his or her website, for example, well enough to tell the difference. But the client's customers will know; their perceptions will affect the client's business; and eventually their response (good or bad) will come back to the translation and localization team in some form.

English-speaking people today expect some degree of English to be used almost everywhere as a lingua franca. People who use any of the major languages—English and French as the working languages of international organizations, Chinese and Spanish as the language of many millions—expect to obtain information in their own languages. The same can be true for Catalan, for Thai, for Malay, for Farsi. They will not settle for awkward, mechanical translation—that will be regarded as an insult. High-quality translation and localization will be necessary features of software, websites and thousands of products. This is one trend that I think will become as basic as the Internet access that propels it: people around this multilingual world will take for granted multilingual information, and the availability of what they want to know in the languages they understand.

About MultiLingual Computing, Inc.

MultiLingual Computing, Inc. is the information source for the localization, internationalization, translation, and language technology industry. Their flagship magazine, MultiLingual Computing & Technology, provides a mix of introductory articles for beginners, linguistic articles for translators, and technical articles for engineers. The free, biweekly e-newsletter, MultiLingual News, offers readers up-to-date information on new products, services, and changes in the industry. MultiLingual's website includes a searchable database of over 1200 industry resources, online articles, listings of events, a blog, and more. MultiLingual Computing, Inc. also co-sponsors the Localization World Conference. For more information, go to **www.multilingual.com**.

Glossary

Translation and Localization Glossary

.BMP (BMP)

A standard bit-mapped graphics format used in Windows. Files end with .BMP extension.

.GIF (GIF)

Graphics Interchange Format. A bit-mapped graphics file format used by the Internet. It features lossless data compression and is best for computer-generated (i.e., nonphotographic) images. Files end with .GIF extension. (See also Lossless.)

.h files

Header files. These are files used in programming (typically C++) to identify and define common items used throughout the program.

JPEG (JPG)

Joint Photographic Experts Group. A lossy compression-type graphics format for color files. Can compress files to 5% of their original size with (some) loss of picture quality. Best for photographic images. Files end with .JPG extension. (See also Lossy.)

.PCX (PCX)

A graphics file format used by PC graphics applications. This widely used file format employs lossless compression. Files end with .PCX extension. (See also Lossless.)

.PDF (PDF)

Portable Document Format. A file format created by Adobe Acrobat, primarily for read-only use with Acrobat Reader. Can be edited with the full version of Acrobat. PDF files capture formatting and layout data from files created with another application, allowing others without that source application to view properly formatted documents via Acrobat Reader on any system supported by Acrobat Reader. Files end with .PDF extension.

.SHG files

Bitmaps with a hotspot overlay. (See also Hotspot.)

.TIFF (TIF)

Tagged Image File Format. Widely used file format for storing bit-mapped images on both PC and Macintosh platforms. Commonly used for scanned images. Files end with .TIF extension.

Active Server Page (ASP)

An HTML page where one or more scripts are processed by an MS server prior to the page being displayed to the user.

ActiveX

A Microsoft program development technology that allows data to be shared among different applications. Conceptually similar to Java, ActiveX has a significant presence in web-based applications.

A-Link

A linking macro provided in WinHelp that allows jumps based on keywords rather than specific context strings. A-links do not have to be localized. A-links are never seen by the end-user and are used only by the help system.

ASCII

American Standard Code for Information Interchange. A standard for assigning numerical values to the set of letters in the Roman alphabet and typographic characters.

BinHex

Binary hexidecimal. A widely-used encoding scheme that converts binary data into ASCII characters. BinHex encoding is especially common on MAC platforms. Files end with .HQX extension.

Bitmap

A graphic for which the color of each pixel is defined by one or more bits (1 bit for black/white, 4 bits for 16 colors, 8 bits for 256 colors, etc.).

Cascading Style Sheets (CSS)

A way of implementing styles in HTML or XML. By combining the styles from several sheets, or using specific rules to override general rules, you can "cascade" the information across multiple pages.

Call out

A small text box referring to an element or feature in a graphic.

Glossary

CAT

Computer Aided Translation is a broad term used to describe computer applications that automate and assist with the act of translating text from one language to another. CAT tools are highly effective in improving translation productivity and quality (e.g. TRADOS Workbench and associated utilities).

Central European (CE) fonts

Specific fonts used for displaying Central and Eastern European languages.

Chunk

Depending on the level at which it is stored, this term is used to describe a subset of content stored in a Content Management System (CMS). A Chunk can be a word, phrase, sentence or paragraph. Chunks are combined by the CMS to create a document. (See also Content Management System.)

CMYK

Cyan Magenta Yellow Black. A color model in which all colors are described as a mixture of these four process colors. CMYK is the standard color model used in offset printing for full-color documents. Also called four-color printing. (See also RGB.)

Compiling

Converting a program written in a high-level programming language from source code into object code. Source code must be compiled before it becomes an executable program.

Computer code

The computer readable code that makes up a program. Also called object code or machine language. (See also Executable.)

Concatenation

A programming method used to avoid creating a number of repetitive messages by starting with a base sentence containing variables that grab the desired elements when the software is run.

Content Management System (CMS)

Tools that automate the process of storing, creating, maintaining, publishing, and updating content. Many variations of CMS tools are currently available in a wide variety of configurations.

Cropping

Trimming the edges of a graphic to make it fit or to remove unwanted sections.

Cultural assessment

Analyzing an individual's cultural preferences through comparative analyses. Allows individuals to acquire the awareness and knowledge necessary for building effective skills and behavioral adaptations for multicultural management and business.

Cultural orientation

Developing cultural self-awareness and effective behavioral strategies to minimize the cultural gaps that occur when contrasting value orientations of different social groups.

Database

An organized collection of data managed by a program that allows users to add, delete, and change the data. (See also DBMS.)

DBE

Double-Byte Enabling. Re-engineering original source code to support the input, display, and manipulation of double-byte language character sets.

DBMS

Database Management System. This program enables users to manage and utilize a database. It is also the interface that facilitates a multi-user system and tracks where data is stored in the storage media so that other programs do not have to.

Decompiling

Opposite of compiling. Changing an application from computer code back into source code. Sometimes referred to as reverse engineering.

Dialog boxes

The rectangular windows used by a program to display information or request information in a Users Interface (UI) (Windows or Mac).

DLL

Dynamic Link Library. A file that contains executable functions or data for applications. Several DLLs come with Windows and are used by many applications, others are written for specific applications. Files end with .DLL extension.

Dots Per Inch (DPI)

A common measurement of resolution used in printing to describe the density of an image or character. Refers to the number of dots of ink a printer is able to print per inch vertically and horizontally. In general, the higher the DPI, the higher the quality of the printed image.

The Guide to Translation and Localization

Glossary

Double-byte character

A character defined with two bytes (16 bits) instead of one byte (8 bits).

Double-byte enabled

A program that can handle double-byte languages. (See also DBE.)

Double-byte languages

Languages that are coded with twice as much information for each character, such as Chinese, Japanese, and Korean.

Drivers

Specialized programs that allow communication between peripherals (printers, scanners, video cards, etc.) and the computer.

Dynamic content

Data or content of a website that is stored in a database and is supplied to the user on the fly, based on what is requested (usually through a form) by the user.

Embedded graphics

A graphic is known as an embedded graphic if all the information for it is stored in a document and not in a separate file. (See also Referenced graphic.)

Exact Match

A term used to describe matching within a translation memory. Also known as 100% match and repetitions, this is a segment stored in the translation memory that is identical to the source segment that is to be translated.

Executable

A program that can be run (executed) on a computer.

FIGS

Abbreviation for the commonly used language set of French, Italian, German, and Spanish.

File Transfer Protocol (FTP)

An alternative to email for transferring files utilizing the Internet. It is often faster and more reliable to use FTP software for large file transfers. Can be accessed using an Internet browser or FTP client software.

Functional QA

Testing of a software application or program to ensure that the localization process does not affect the functionality of the software and that the content displays correctly on the screen.

Fuzzy logic

A logic that allows the concept of partial truth-truth values between "completely true" and "completely false." Used to create near matches instead of exact matches during searches, and in artificial intelligence programs.

Fuzzy match

A term used to describe matching within a translation memory. A segment that is similar (but not identical) to the sentence or phrase the translator is currently translating.

G11N

See Globalization.

Globalization

The process of conceptualizing a product line for the global marketplace so that it can be sold anywhere in the world with only minor revision. It is most easily thought of as a global marketing strategy and is associated with all marketing concepts (branding, establishing market share, etc.). Globalization is particularly important in consumer industries such as clothing and food.

Glossary

A list of terms which includes extensive definitions and grammatical configurations. (See also Terminology list.)

GUI

The part of a software application that is visible to the end-user. Stands for Graphical User Interface.

Hotspot

The part of a graphic in a hypertext document that, when clicked on, jumps to another location. Similar to a hypertext link.

HTML

Hyper Text Markup Language. A coding system used on the Internet to format text and set up hyperlinks between documents. Similar to SGML.

Glossary

HTMLHelp

A Microsoft Help system format based on HTML.

I18N

See Internationalization.

Integration testing (Interoperability)

Confirmation that two or more systems (computers, communication devices, networks, software, and other information technology components) are able to interact with one another and exchange data according to a prescribed method in order to achieve predictable results. (ISO ITC-215.)

International brand development

The process of giving a product the look and feel of having been developed in the target country. Requires that a brand or message be clear, easily identifiable, and culturally acceptable to the target market. A successful brand can be conveyed clearly and concisely, regardless of the language or writing source.

Internationalization

The process of engineering a product so it can be localized for export to any country.

Interpretation

Translation of spoken words from one language to another. Usually the interpreter waits until the first speaker has finished a phrase or sentence before translating. Simultaneous interpretation occurs when the interpreter translates the speech as it is being given. The skill set of an interpreter is different than that of a translator.

ISO

International Organization for Standardization. A world wide federation of national standards bodies from approximately 130 countries.

Java

A platform-independent, object-oriented programming language. Java can add animation, spreadsheets, and information processing features that HTML cannot provide.

Kerning

The space between two text characters. (See also Tracking.)

K-link

A linking macro provided in WinHelp that allows jumps based on keywords rather than specific context strings. K-links require translation.

L10N

See Localization.

Leading

The space between two or more lines of text. Also called line spacing.

Leverage

Building current translation projects on those previously completed. Reduces the need to retranslate words and phrases previously translated. The process of using one translation for repeated sections of text.

Localization

Adapting a software, document, or website product to various markets or localities. This may require a variety of steps including translating user interface text, modifying formats for numbers and dates, and replacing culturally inappropriate graphics or system design.

Localization engineering

The process of using specific localization applications, compilers, and tools to prepare software for release in other markets or localities.

Lossless

A term used to describe compression techniques that don't lose any data. Lossless compression techniques usually reduce the size of the compressed file up to 50% of the original file.

Lossy

A term used to describe compression techniques that lose some data or details. Commonly used with graphics and video. Lossy compression techniques can compress files to around 5% of their original size with some loss of data.

Multilingual print production

Producing packaging, advertising, and related collateral in multiple languages for simultaneous release.

Multiterm

An application made by TRADOS to point out already translated terminology to translators.

New text

A term used to describe matching within a translation memory. Text where the source segments being translated do not correspond to any of the target segments.

The Guide to Translation and Localization —— 119

Glossary

Online content

Any written content that is intended for publishing via a network or the Internet. While online content can most often be printed if the user desires, the format is often not optimized for specific layout specifications.

Online user interface

A software product/service that is delivered to the user via a network or the Internet. This software does not reside or run on a 'local' machine.

Pixel

Picture Element. One dot on a computer screen. The smallest image-forming unit on a display screen.

Quality assurance

The process of assuring that the target document resembles the source document as closely as possible. The process can include, for example, verification of layout and graphics to confirm the document is complete.

Referenced graphic

A graphic that appears in a document in which the information for the graphic is stored in a separate file and minimal information about the graphic is stored in the actual document. (See also Embedded graphics.)

Resizing

During localization, software strings may expand and no longer fit within the dimensions of the source dialogs, buttons, menus, etc. When this occurs, engineers use specialized software to resize the UI elements so that the text fits within the allocated area.

Resource files

Source files that contain information to be compiled into the program. They contain the parts of the application that is seen by the user. Typical file types include: .rc, .res, .bmp, .ico, .cur.

RGB

Red Green Blue. Blending these three colors allows computer monitors to display color images. (See also CMYK.)

RoboHelp

An application made by eHelp. RoboHelp assists in writing help files using Microsoft Word.

RTF

Rich Text Format. A type of document that encodes formatting as text-based tags. Can be opened as text to view the tags or converted to look like a Word document (without the tags visible). Used as a source file for WinHelp.

Scaling

Changing the size of a graphic so that no distortion occurs.

Screen shots

A graphic image of what is seen on the computer screen. Often used in user's manuals to show how an application looks on the screen. Also called "screencaps," "screen captures" or "SCAPS."

SEA

Self Extracting Archive. A file that decompresses itself. Used on a Mac OS.

Segment

The basic unit of source text, as identified by a translation tool, that can be aligned with a corresponding translation from the translation memory. A segment is commonly defined as the content from one paragraph break to the next, usually a sentence, but a segment can be a header, items in a list, cells in a table, a paragraph, etc. (See also Translation memory.)

SGML

Standard Generalized Markup Language. SGML is an ISO standard for marking text files to show how they should be formatted. HTML is a specialized application of SGML rules.

Single-sourcing

A method of using one source of stored content to generate multiple types of documents on multiple platforms. (See also Content Management System.)

Sizing

Changing the dimensions of an image or graphic. Sizing can cause distortion or loss of image quality. (See also Scaling.)

Source code

The human-readable code that is compiled to make a program. Some types of source code are C++, Java, and Visual Basic.

Glossary

Source file

A file containing the source material that is used to create the translated product during a localization project. (See also Source code.)

String tags

Tags used in strings to mark where something will be added. For Example: "%s" = another string, "/n" = a return character, and "/t" = a tab, etc.

Strings

Groupings of characters (letters, numbers, and/or punctuation marks) that are used in programs such as error messages, button labels, etc. Often strings are enclosed in single or double quotes. Strings need to be translated if they contain text that will be seen by the user.

Style sheet

A document or template that defines the style and layout of a document. Contains instructions for margins, fonts, page size, spacing, etc. Aids in the consistent appearance of pages in a large document. Also known as a style guide.

Terminology list

The terminology list is created as a reference for linguists (translators), and is usually specific to a project. It provides the linguists with the English source word and the target language equivalent. Terminology lists are created by the linguists and approved by the client prior to translation. A list of terms and descriptions are recommended for each specific case. (See also Glossary.)

Text expansion

The increase in the total number of characters that often occurs during translation.

Text extraction

Manually or electronically pulling text out of a source file (Quark, Illustrator, PDF) and placing it into a Word file for use by a linguist.

Tracking

The average space between characters in a block of text.

TRADOS® Translator's Workbench

An application that assists a translator by showing how similarly translated sentences were translated. This software program is used to store linguist-translated text and display it when previously translated phrases appear in a word file. Helps to assure consistency and reduce redundant work.

Translation

The process of converting written material from a source language into a target language.

Translation memory (TM)

A database in which previous translations and corresponding source text are stored for future use. New source text is automatically paired with these prior translations through the use of database technology. The matching process identifies new text, fuzzy matches and 100% matches and repetitions. The linguist uses the Workbench to manage this process. (See also TRADOS Translator's Workbench.)

Translation unit (TU)

A single segment pair of source and translated text stored in the translation memory.

Unicode

A platform-independent character set that attempts to unify all character sets into one 16-bit character set. Unicode is a two-byte encoding that allows for 65,536 (256 times 256) code points and includes all major alphabetic languages plus a unified Chinese, Japanese, and Korean character set.

Verification testing

Confirmation of any testable requirement, including functional testing of hardware and software system components, compatibility testing of one component to another, design verification, compliance to industry standards, and third party interoperability.

WinHelp

Short for Windows Help file. WinHelp is also the name of the application that runs Windows help files (.hlp).

XML

XML is the acronym for eXtensible Markup Language. This is a universally accepted format for creating and tagging documents and data for display on the Internet. It was developed, and is administered, by the World Wide Web Consortium (W3C). (See also HTML and SGML.)

Zip file

A compressed file created by the utility application PKzip or WinZip on a PC.

Resources

RESOURCES	
European Union	http://europa.eu.int
International Trade Administration, Department of Commerce • FREE telephone consulting with international trade counselors	800-USA-TRADE http://www.ita.doc.gov/
U.S. Bureau of the Census, Center for International Business Research	301-457-1722 www.census.gov/foreign-trade/www/
U.S. Chamber of Commerce International	1-202-659-6000 http://www.uschamber.org/default.htm
U.S. Department of Commerce • For export advice contact: http://export.gov/ • "Basic Guide to Exporting" (http://www.unzco.com/basicguide/index.html)	1-800-USA-TRADE http://home.doc.gov/

ASSOCIATIONS	
American Society for Testing and Materials (ASTM) 100 Barr Harbor Drive West Conshohocken, PA 19428-2959	610-832-9585 www.astm.org
American Translators Association Reinekers Lane, Suite 590 Alexandria, VA 22314	703-683-6100 www.atanet.org
LISA Localisation Industry Standards Association 7, route de Monastère CH-1173 Féchy, Switzerland	+41 21 821 3210 www.lisa.org
Society for Technical Communication (STC) 901 North Stuart St., #904 Arlington, VA 22203-1854	703-522-4114 www.stc.org
Software Information and Industry Association 1090 Vermont Ave, NW, Sixth Floor Washington, DC 20005	202-289-7442 www.siia.net

INTERNATIONAL COMPUTER SOCIETIES	
Australia	www.acs.org.au
Austria	www.ocg.or.at
Belgium	www.bfia.be
Brazil	www.sbc.org.br
Canada	www.cips.ca
China	www.cie-china.org
Czech Republic	www.cs.cas.cz
France	www.asti.asso.fr

Resources

Germany	www.gi-ev.de
Hong Kong	www.hkcs.org.hk
Hungary	www.njszt.iif.hu
India	www.csi-india.org
Ireland	www.ics.ie
Israel	www.iash.org.il
Italy	www.a-i-p.it/index.php
Japan	www.ipsj.or.jp
Korea	www.kiss.or.kr
Netherlands	www.ngi.nl
New Zealand	www.nzcs.org.nz
Norway	www.dnd.no
Philippines	www.pcs-it.org
Russia	www.ras.ru
Singapore	www.scs.org.sg
Spain	www.dit.upm.es
Switzerland	www.s-i.ch/
United Kingdom	www.bcs.org.uk

PUBLICATIONS	
ATA Chronicle • Publication of the American Translators Association	703-683-6100 www.atanet.org
Intercom • Publication of the Society for Technical Communication	703-522-4114 www.stc.org
J@pan Inc. • Website with useful information about doing business in Japan.	www.japaninc.net

MultiLingual Computing, Inc.
319 North First Street
Sandpoint, ID 83864
  • **MultiLingual Computing and Technology**
    Publication of record for the Translation and Localization industries.
  • **MultiLingual News**
    Daily updates with industry news on the Internet.
  • **Latecomer's Guide to the New Europe**
    A handy and concise pamphlet geared to firms interested in expanding their market into Europe.
	208-263-8178
	www.multilingual.com
	info@multilingual.com

Software Business 7355 E. Orchard #100 Englewood, CO 80111	720-528-3770 www.softwarebusinessonline.com
Technical Communication – • Journal of the Society for Technical Communications	703-522-4114 www.techcomm-online.org

Contact Info

Single-Source Content Management (Chapter 14)
AuthorIT Software Corporation
P.O. Box 200-273
Albany, Auckland
New Zealand
Ph: +64 (9) 915 5070
Fax: +64 (9) 915 5071
Email: info@author-it.com
www.author-it.com
Local resellers are available throughout the world.

But They Speak English, Right? (Chapter 15)
Brandfluency℠
3820 150th Avenue NE
Redmond, WA 98052
Ph: 425-882-9212
Fax: 425-881-8377
Email: info@brandfluency.com
www.brandfluency.com

Translation and Localization Today, Tomorrow, and the Day After (Chapter 18)
MultiLingual Computing, Inc.
319 North First Avenue
Sandpoint, ID 83864
Ph: 208-263-8178
Fax: 208-263-6310
Email: info@multilingual.com
www.multilingual.com

Testing and Integration of Software and Hardware (Chapter 16)
PCTest Corporation
4950 NE 148th Avenue
Portland, OR 97230
Ph: 503-257-8000
Fax: 503-257-8835
Email: info@pctest.com
www.pctest.com

Cultural Training and Awareness (Chapter 17)
Training Management Corporation
600 Alexander Road
Princeton, NJ 08540
Ph: 609-951-0525
Fax: 609-951-0395
Email: info@tmcorp.com
www.tmcorp.com

Lingo Systems
15115 SW Sequoia Parkway
Suite 200
Portland, OR 97224
Ph: 503-419-4856
Toll Free: 800-878-8523
Fax: 503-419-4873
Email: info@lingosys.com
www.lingosys.com